RID

Also by Deborah Meroff

Footsteps in The Sea

Riding The Storm

More Adventures
With Operation Mobilisation

Deborah Meroff

Hodder & Stoughton
LONDON SYDNEY AUCKLAND

*To my faithful partners, who have followed
me around the world these dozen years
with their prayers, love and support.*

Scripture quotations are taken from the HOLY BIBLE, NEW
INTERNATIONAL VERSION, copyright © 1973, 1978, 1984
by the International Bible Society. Used by permission.

First published in Great Britain 1996

The right of Deborah Meroff to be identified as the Author of
the Work has been asserted by her in accordance with the
Copyright, Designs and Patents Act 1988.

10 9 8 7 6 5 4 3 2 1

British Library Cataloguing in Publication Data
A record for this book is available from the British Library

ISBN 0 340 67859 3

Typeset by Hewer Text Composition Services, Edinburgh
Printed and bound in Great Britain by
Cox & Wyman Ltd, Reading, Berks.

Hodder and Stoughton Ltd
A Division of Hodder Headline PLC
338 Euston Road
London NW1 3BH

God works in a mysterious way
His wonders to perform;
He plants his footsteps in the Sea
And rides upon the Storm.

William Cowper

Contents

Foreword

Debbie Meroff is a full-time writer with Operation Mobilisation. She spends, on average, six to nine months of the year travelling. These travels are often in difficult, and occasionally dangerous, areas.

Why does Debbie live like this? She has a driving ambition to get the message of what God is doing around this world to as many people as possible.

In this book you will travel through many parts of God's world with Debbie. You will be amazed at her resourcefulness and perseverance, through thick and thin, 'to get the story'. You will also find cause to give great praise to God for what He is doing in His world, and no doubt be challenged by all that remains to be done. I pray that as you read you will be motivated to even greater commitment to the task which is at the very heart of the calling of the church.

Peter Maiden
Carlisle

1

Journey to the centre of the earth

'Well, what do you think? Are you ready for Central Asia?'

I caught my photographer friend's grin and felt a leap of excitement. It was 1992, and the vast territory which had been known as the Soviet Union was still breaking up, like ice feeling the first warmth of spring. One by one the republics were drifting away to experience a life of their own. Almost overnight the USSR had become the Commonwealth of Independent States.

For most people Central Asia might as well be a black hole. A few might remember Marco Polo and Ghengis Khan. But even if those explorers were to re-visit the Silk Road these days, they would find themselves disorientated. The camels and caravans and legendary conquerors have long vanished, along with most of the other exotic trappings of the Mysterious East. They have been ground to dust by time, by earthquakes, and perhaps most cruelly of all by the iron heel of Russia.

Central Asians who dared to resist the invasion of the tsars, and later the Soviets, were driven out to the vast, windswept steppes to starve or freeze. Stalin massacred untold thousands. Huge numbers of Russians were then resettled in the region to dilute the ethnic population. The Russian language was imposed on the culture along with Russian-style education and architecture. Immense, identically drab buildings rose in methodically laid-out cities. Communism became the way of life. But now, suddenly, the invader's heel had been removed. Native Kazaks, Kirghiz, Uzbeks, Turkmen and Tajiks were standing up and surveying their newly liberated lands with a stirring of wonder and pride. At long last they were free to re-establish their own official languages, religions, cultures – if only they could remember what they were! Independence in Central Asia had brought the best of times and the worst of times. Was there really life for them after Lenin?

It was time to go there, and find out.

Operation Mobilisation photographer Tim Wright and I made plans to rendezvous with a third OMer, Rosemary Hack, in Alma-Ata, the capital of Kazakstan. The new republics did not yet have embassies of their own in London so we applied for visas through the Russian embassy. This turned out to be a major character-building exercise, requiring great determination in pushing one's way through the crowd at the gates and into the building before the door closed. As it was we only succeeded in getting a Kazakstan visa before flying into Moscow's international airport in early October.

In Russia it was already winter: a light dusting of snow lay on the ground. When the local man who was supposed to meet us failed to appear, we realised we'd have to find our own way to the domestic airport. Domodiedova was inconveniently situated on the other side of the city, a good 100 kilometres distant. With no shuttle buses, we had only one option. A sea of taxi drivers (controlled by the Mafia, we'd been told) knew it too, and circled like sharks. They would only deal in American dollars, but Tim proved himself a canny negotiator. We were soon on our way through the outskirts of Moscow.

A traveller's fact sheet had warned, 'Domodiedova airport is at best crowded and confusing. It is comparable to a provincial airport in a third-world country and in bad need of replacement. There are no signs to direct you, so you will have to find your own way.' We actually did see signs, but they were all in Russian. The country was clearly not yet geared up to receiving tourists. The few amenities available in the international airport were completely dispensed with in the domestic airport. The place looked like a prisoner of war camp with people strewn everywhere, all guarding heaps of baggage of every conceivable description. After some bewildered wandering we eventually stumbled over the Intourist transit lounge. Interior decoration was obviously not a priority here either, but there were some dilapidated seats. The toilets had to be avoided until the point of desperation.

During the wait for our connecting flight we met a group of Chinese from a Baptist church in Los Angeles, also bound for Alma-Ata, a Korean couple who were hoping to plant a church, and four young Americans from Campus Crusade who were going to pioneer a team at the university in Bishkek, Kirgistan, for a year. The students had been waiting for their flight all day and fell with glee on the pack of Uno cards I produced. When their plane was ready we saw them off, never expecting to meet up again. But we did!

According to my traveller's tips, Aeroflot was the largest airline in the world because it had a monopoly on the Commonwealth of Independent States:

The Soviet airline is a once-in-a-lifetime experience not to be missed. Seats are marked with Russian letters, so it takes a little practice to find the right place at first. When you find your place someone else may already be sitting there, so just find an empty seat. The toilets are always in the rear and have been used at times by some unlucky passengers in the past as substitute seats for an entire flight. You will notice there is none of the excellent service, standard safety briefings, or friendly chit-chat from the pilot and crew to which we have become accustomed in the West. There is a conspicous 'take it or leave it' attitude. Delays or flight cancellations are not uncommon or unexpected.

Our flight left towards midnight. The passengers were herded outside to stand in the falling snow for some time until a broken-down bus took us out to the plane. Although we had been given seat numbers, all courtesies were ignored and everyone pushed and shoved their way aboard, every man for himself. Fortunately Tim and I ended up with seats together. The plane appeared to be left over from World War Two. My seatbelt was permanently adjusted to fit the girth of a very fat person and some people didn't bother to buckle up at all. We relaxed only when the aircraft made it off the ground. 'Did Aeroflot serve meals?' we wondered. Tim and I had missed lunch and supper and were ravenous enough to eat just about anything. When the flight attendant started handing out trays, however, we looked at each other and burst into hysterical laughter. Our meals consisted of a third of a slice of brown bread, a small, pale lump of processed chicken, plus one very stale biscuit. We donated our portions to another passenger who gladly accepted all offerings. Our scowling flight attendant, who could have

4

passed for a prison warden, disappeared after collecting the trays. We weren't graced with her presence again for the remainder of the trip.

I was not prepared for the beauty that greeted us in Kazakstan. Splendid snow-draped peaks rose all around us, poetically called the Tien-Shan, 'Celestial Mountains'; these formed a natural border with China. Alma-Ata itself (now Almaty) nestled in a valley. The name of the city meant 'Father of Apples' and the hillsides were planted with ten million trees. Each year farms harvested not only apples but pears, lemons, melons, apricots and pomegranates. The worm in the apple of this idyllic setting was the area's tendency to occasional flooding from glacier run-off, avalanches and earthquakes. Preventative measures had minimised these natural disasters. The problems were now mostly man-made. The Soviets had given little thought to pollution control in their industrial plans and the glorious mountain vista was often shrouded in smog.

I didn't really know what I expected Central Asia to look like, but Alma-Ata wasn't it. The city was like a depressed Eastern Europe, without colour or character. Streets were laid out in a grid and occupied by endless grey blocks of apartment and office buildings. Only the trees dressed in rich autumn shades, and the occasional glimpses of onion-domed churches lent the landscape some variety and life.

Our OM representative in Kazakstan, Tom Webb, had arranged for a twenty-year-old Russian named Slava to serve as our translator and guide. Slava was a physics student at Alma-Ata University, who two years before had traded his atheism for a strong faith in Christ. Slava's English was practically accent-free. He also possessed a wonderful sense of humour, so the four of us got along very well.

5

For the first few days I shared the flat of an American named Lee Taylor. Lee had been in the country for about a year and, although a Christian, she was not a missionary in the traditional sense. She was a businesswoman who intended to make a profit; but at the same time she wanted to use her skills to help the Kazak people get on their feet financially. 'Islamic countries are sending bankers, investors, and entrepreneurs to Central Asia,' she explained to me. 'They know the power of solid business relationships. When God calls Christians to the marketplace we are his ministers to the world through our business. No culture is as desperate for values as the former Soviet Union. My hope is that godly people will pour millions of dollars' worth of profitable investment into Kazakstan, and prove to a drifting people the providential love of God.'

I was impressed by her reasoning. Kazakstan stretched a million miles from the Caspian Sea to China, big enough to contain all of Britain, France, Spain, Germany, Denmark and Sweden within its borders. The land overflowed with natural resources. Although it could no longer depend on Russia for fuel or manufactured goods, there was enough potential for this giant to stand on its own. First, however, the republic had to have finance and technology to build the infrastructure. For anyone with expertise in transportation, communications, and industry, this was a land of opportunity.

But what about the man on the street? When I remarked to Lee about the well-dressed appearance of the average man and woman, she smiled. 'Appearances are deceptive. The truth is people own only that one good outfit – perhaps two – which they wear every day until it is worn out.'

Most residents struggled on a day-to-day basis. All were deeply anxious about surviving their country's transition to a market economy. The ruble that bore the image of Lenin was worth less each day; all the republics were talking about establishing their own currencies. A loaf of bread that cost a half ruble only a year ago was now sold for fifteen to twenty rubles. The food shops featured rows of empty shelves; people stood in endless queues for basic items and some paid other people to wait for them. I discovered that cleaning products and washing-up liquid were among the scarce items: I had to wash dishes in Lee's flat with baking soda. Toilet paper was also on the most-wanted list. Instructed to buy any we found in the market, we purchased rolls of paper that had the consistency of adding machine tape. The toilet refused to swallow it.

It was the elderly I felt most sorry for. Money they had put by to keep them in old age was now worthless. Slava told us his grandmother received the equivalent of eight dollars' support a month. We saw many pensioners sweeping the streets, selling fruit or simply begging. Only vodka flowed in abundance, and the only people who seemed to be flourishing were the Mafia. Tales of their reign of terror were multiplying. While we were in Alma-Ata a woman was hacked to death because she refused to pay 'protection money' for her kiosk.

Tim, Slava, Rose and I often found ourselves gravitating toward the *shashlik* sellers on the streets whenever hunger struck. The mouth-watering aroma of skewered beef or lamb barbecued over charcoal was impossible to resist. The four of us could also fill up for less than three dollars in a hotel that used to serve as the Communist party headquarters. The doorman was singularly unfriendly and tried to keep us out by insisting the restaurant was closed. We couldn't understand this attitude and took it as a challenge to outwit him. The only time we went up to the 26th floor restaurant of the modern Hotel Kazakstan was to take some panoramic shots of the city. The first 'World Congress of Spiritual Concord' was being held in the hotel at the time. Hari Krishna, Moonies, Bahais, Orthodox Russian priests, and Muslims from around the world were paying $100 per head to attend. Some Hari Krishna devotees singing in the restaurant invited us to visit their temple down the street.

Cult followers and Muslim missionaries were taking full advantage of the comparative freedom of religion in Kazakstan. The atheism enforced by Russian occupiers was only skin deep for many men and women – most were now looking for something to fill the void. Muslims were loud in proclaiming that the Kazak culture was rooted in Islam, an important point for people who wanted their own identity. As the country's forty per cent Russian population showed more and more interest in Christianity, there was a real danger the two people groups would be polarised. In fact Kazakstan's 130 churches were made up almost entirely of Russians.

Slava's church, New Life, had been operating for only two years at the time we attended it. In the last six months numbers had doubled and they now averaged 500 to 700 for services. Another Sunday we visited a thriving Korean church. According to Lee Taylor, Stalin had forcefully exiled large groups of Koreans from Northern Manchuria to Kazakstan. There were now fifteen Korean churches for the country's half million Korean population. The congregation we saw was mixed with about 300 Russians and Koreans. The service was conducted in both languages and many native Koreans actually attended, Lee told us, in order to learn better Korean. Later we visited an orphanage and learned this church was the only group that took an interest in the children. Many had become Christians as a result.

Russian was still the universal language in Central Asia. We found eager takers whenever we offered Russian Scriptures, but it was only a matter of time before Kazak became the nation's first choice. Ten million people already spoke the language. Yet only a handful of Christian workers were studying it, and only half of the New Testament was as yet translated into Kazak. I visited the home of the German couple who were committed to the project. They worked long hours every day and except for the help of a Kazak couple, they worked alone. 'Ideally we will finish the New Testament in two years,' they said, 'but it's not in our hands. The Kazak couple who work with us are not believers. They have been criticised and there is growing pressure from Muslims. If we had to find new translators, we would lose half a year.'

The books of the Bible were printed locally as they were completed, and as funds became available. Unfortunately, while we were there, the Mafia beat up a local believer connected with the work and took $5,000 which had been earmarked for the printing of Luke's Gospel. When it came time for Tim, Rose and I to travel to Tashkent we went by way of Chimkent and, at Tom Webb's request, dropped off a delivery of Scriptures.

Chimkent lay on the southern border of Kazakstan, strategically close to both Uzbekistan and Tajikistan. The city wasn't much to look at. Its chief claim to fame was that the local lead factory had been responsible for producing eight out of ten of the former USSR's bullets. But the warmth of the welcome we received from our contact Misha and his family made up for it. Misha, whose woolly beard and stocky frame made him resemble Father Christmas, met us off the train and loaded the books we'd brought into his car. He was full of energy and enthusiasm and impatient to show us his church.

Misha's pride in the church was justified. As we walked around the building he told us how the members had waited seventeen years for permission to build it. They had spent the last three years lovingly putting it up with their own hands. This Baptist church was the only one in a city with ninety-four mosques. Eight hundred people gathered here each Sunday to worship. Misha then took us back to his home, where his wife and daughters had prepared an extravagant meal in our honour. Our host had been an engineer in the days before independence but now he was a dedicated Gideon representative for the area. His heart's desire was to see Central Asians exposed to God's love before it was too late. 'Islam is moving fast – we may have already lost Tajikistan. And if they can take Chimkent, they can take all of Kazakstan.' While we spoke the telephone rang. Someone was offering Misha the chance to start Bible clubs in fifteen different school locations. He shook his head as he hung up and gave us a rueful smile. 'If you sent me twenty missionaries, in one month we could start twenty churches.'

All too soon it was time to say goodbye to our new friends, and resume our journey. We didn't have far to go. Within about two hours we had crossed the border into Uzbekistan and were rolling into the centuries-old focus of the caravan trade, Tashkent.

2

Unravelling the silk road

Tashkent received its name, meaning 'Stone City,' with good reason. The foundation of rock that lies under the capital has been responsible for a long history of earthquakes, including one that levelled the city in 1966. But tremors from the breakup of the Soviet Union had shaken the republic even more. Lenin's statue was now missing from the main square and a golden globe bearing a map of Uzbekistan stood in its place. But the government was still Communist in all but name.

We were met at the bus terminal by Johan, one of the Christian workers we'd come to interview. As we travelled across the city to an empty flat he had arranged for us to stay in, I tried to pick out the Uzbek population from the Russians. It wasn't difficult – Uzbek men almost universally sported a square black and white embroidered cap, and many also wore black baggy trousers and long boots. Their women were set apart by colourful headscarves and peasant skirts. Russian residents, on the other hand, flaunted conspicuously European fashions and modern hairstyles.

Tashkent had been rebuilt after the 1966 earthquake in the usual Russian style with wide avenues and unimaginative buildings. The city was, however, far more modern and attractive than Alma-Ata, with its flashes of blue-domed mosques and outdoor markets giving the place character. Tashkent has Central Asia's only subway system. Although overcrowded, the service is modern and efficient, and the metro tickets cost only a fraction of a penny.

Like most of the former Soviet republics, the people who lived here were used to a dual language society. Russian was still the lingua franca, but Uzbeks were increasingly demanding the use of their native tongue. Russian street signs had already been replaced by Uzbek signs, and Uzbek was now the language taught in school.

Tashkent is sometimes called Central Asia's spiritual capital. It certainly had an altogether more Islamic atmosphere than the republic we had just left. We saw Korans being sold along with other books in the streets, and new mosques in the process of being built. Islam's crescent even figured on the national flag. A foreign businessman told us that fundamentalists were pressing for Islamic rule, but the present government was taking a hard line against all religion. They wouldn't even accept money from Saudi Arabia because it had strings attached.

Compared to enthusiastic Muslim efforts to woo the populace, Christians were not making much of a mark. Until a few years ago there were perhaps two foreign workers in the whole country; now there were about a hundred, but they were still groping their way through restrictions. Newcomers had to be highly motivated to stick it out in this isolated place. Most Christians came as teachers, medical workers or business professionals and their evangelism efforts were strictly undercover – the film *Jesus* had been banned after one mission showed it without discretion. Phones were routinely tapped. And although accommodation was cheap – $100 for a modest apartment,

$200 for a very nice two or three bedroom flat – it was hard to find. The government was making things tougher by requiring foreigners to stay in hotels or dormitories. 'We've seen people come here short term and go home disappointed,' one young couple told us. 'Their expectations were wrong. This place is not oriental, it's Russian: big office blocks and faceless apartment buildings. It's not fun to live in Tashkent. You really have to know the Lord wants you here.' A wife and mother observed, 'The Soviet mentality is cautious, suspicious and hard. There is an oppressive feeling here. You notice the rudeness, pushing and shoving on the street. Medical care is poor. Abortions are the accepted method of birth control. Women go through an average of seven abortions in their lifetime!'

I was pleased to meet up unexpectedly with a former *Doulos* shipmate. Aglae was Venezuelan and she was teaching Spanish under the auspices of another mission. She agreed that living in Tashkent wasn't easy – particularly for single women. 'It's lonely. There's not much to do for recreation, plus it's not safe to go out at night. Shopping is a big adjustment too. Everything takes forever! You get ration cards for basics like tea and sugar, and coupons for the state store. Nothing is available on a consistent basis.'

For in-and-out visitors like Rose and me, however, the prospect of shopping was irresistible. The colourful spice market and bazaars might have been straight from the Silk Road days. To Tim they were a photographer's dream. One friendly Uzbek trader who he captured on film insisted on presenting us with a melon. We all succumbed to the traditional hats, scarves, and hand-embroidered wall hangings. Although the sellers expected us to bargain with them, it made us feel guilty – the prices were incredibly low to start with. I was trying to exercise some restraint until I fell in love with a hand-painted Russian samovar in the state department store. My Ukrainian grandmother had owned a tea urn just like it. When Rose found out it was only $10 she decided she had to have one too – the tourist shop at the Hotel Tashkent sold the same thing for over $100! The problem of how on earth we would transport our treasures only stopped us momentarily. The samovar was something we simply had to have. And somehow we managed it.

While we were looking around in the store a woman edged up, offering to sell her ration coupons. Others like her stood outside the store while more still were trying to trade rubles for dollars. It was the same everywhere we went in Central Asia. People were coping any way they could with rocketing inflation and a plunging ruble.

One evening Rose and I splashed out on the ballet. The programme was of course in Russian and we didn't even know what we were watching, philistines that we were! But although neither of us were avid ballet enthusiasts we did enjoy the dancers' professional performance and the live orchestra – all for the sum of five pennies each! We both remarked on the large number of teenagers in attendance. Our western cultures might offer a wider choice of amusements to young people, but quantity isn't always quality.

Samarkand. The very name of this 'Eden of the East' summons exotic images in most peoples' imagination. When Tim decided he had to take photographs of the legendary city Rose and I didn't discourage him. Unfortunately our driver was slow enough and our vehicle small enough to qualify for the Guinness Book of Records, and the three-hour journey ended up taking five hours each way. But it was worth it. The great conqueror Tamerlane had made the oasis-city his personal headquarters back in the

1400s. The lavishly beautiful mosques, madrasas (schools) and tombs he built were now largely restored, and to wander through the courtyards of these buildings was to be transported backward in time. Muslim visitors outside several of the tombs were actually praying and leaving offerings for the dead. Tamerlane's own resting place was adorned with striking blue mosaics which he had obviously ensured were the finest of all. The man's success as a campaigner was only exceeded by his cruelty. In Afghanistan, he had once made a tower out of 2,000 live men and cemented them together with bricks and clay while they were still living.

Travelling between Tashkent and Samarkand we noticed mile after mile devoted to cotton fields. Cotton was the 'white gold' of Uzbekistan, providing 70 per cent of the total yield of the CIS. But the republic also claimed the world's largest gold mine. Bek, the Uzbek student who translated for us, commented, 'The Russians took our gold. Now life is better – we can do what we want!'

After five days in Uzbekistan Johan helped us make arrangements to head back to Kazakstan. While we were waiting on the station platform, ready to depart, an official suddenly appeared, demanding to see our passports and tickets. My heart sank – Rose was the only one of us who possessed an Uzbekistan visa as Tim and I hadn't been able to obtain one from the Russian Embassy in London. Tom had assured us that travel between the new republics was no problem. The official, however, saw it otherwise and seized the chance to interrogate us. Where had we been staying in Tashkent? Why hadn't we been in a hotel like other visitors? How had we managed to pay for our train tickets in rubles instead of dollars? The man ordered us to follow him to his office. Rose boldly declined, saying she would stay with the luggage. We'd had difficulty enough hauling it through the crowds in the first place. Naturally I insisted on remaining with her – some bystanders had been eyeing our bags with altogether too much interest, and it was unsafe for Rose to be left alone. Tim took our passports and went off with the man while Rose and I began some earnest praying. Other people were starting to board the train and we were just beginning to fear the worst when Tim strode down the platform, grinning broadly. The official had wanted sixty dollars but he had talked him down to forty. A 'fine,' the official called it, but the money almost certainly went into his pocket.

We flung ourselves and our baggage onto the train and found our compartment. Praise God, we thought. Nothing to do now but get through the tedium of an overnight journey. Johan had inquired and said we would reach Alma-Ata at nine o'clock – the next morning, we assumed. We ate the snacks we'd brought along, played Uno, and then stretched out to catch whatever sleep we could. Next morning we were up early and ready to go, anxious not to miss our stop as all station signs and announcements were in Russian. Eight thirty arrived, then nine o'clock. When nine thirty passed with no sign of our destination we began to panic. 'Alma-Ata?' we repeated like idiots, collaring every passenger we could find. They only shrugged. No one could speak English. Finally another passenger took pity on our agitated condition and pointed to his watch. Painstakingly he traced the hands circling the watch in another entire revolution, to 9 p.m. 'Alma-Ata,' he said, smiling. The light dawned. We had another twelve whole hours to go!

How could it possibly take that long to get to Kazakstan? we asked ourselves. We soon found out. 'I love to see it lap the miles and lick the valleys up,' the poet Emily Dickinson once enthused about the iron horse. Obviously she wasn't describing the Central Asian variety. Our train crawled over the barren steppes with the reluctance of a snail, coming thankfully to a halt wherever there was any excuse of habitation. With absolutely nothing in the prairie-like landscape to engage our interest we were soon out of our minds with boredom. We were also very hungry, having consumed all our food the afternoon and evening before. The train's passenger comforts did not extend to food – they only grudgingly made provision for the most basic of nature's demands. The toilets were in fact so appalling we had to steel ourselves to use them.

By mid-afternoon we had exhausted every possible topic of conversation and closed our eyes again, hoping to lose consciousness. Tim had actually succeeded in falling asleep when an official knocked, entered, and indicated he wanted to see our passports. I stiffened without actually opening my eyes. This was it, I thought. The man would discover that Tim and I had no visas for Uzbekistan, and we'd be fined again or maybe worse. Rose stirred languidly and handed him her passport, which did have a visa. Then she indicated her prostrate companions and shrugged helplessly. The official hesitated. 'I come back,' he announced finally, and shut the door. Rose and I looked at each other and laughed nervously. 'What on earth are we going to do?' I said. 'I don't know,' Rose replied, 'Let's pray. Maybe he won't come back.' We entreated the Lord while Tim slept blissfully on. The man didn't return.

It grew dark. We had by now ascertained that our train was ultimately bound for Siberia; the information made us understandably paranoid about getting off. Alma-Ata had several different stops, so we took the first one and telephoned Tom to come and pick us up. Apparently we'd got off at the wrong station so it was a long wait, and very cold. Rose and I left our bags with Tim and went inside to stand out of the wind. Three young men weaved up to us, obviously drunk, and suggested something in Russian. When ignoring them had no effect we decided to rejoin Tim. The men followed us, and two of them started harassing Tim to exchange rubles for dollars. The atmosphere was quickly turning nasty and while the two of them were engaged, the third man suddenly made an obscene approach to Rose. Rose is blonde and attractive, and after living in the Middle East she had a great deal of experience in fending off unwanted advances. She smacked the Russian across the face. He unhesitatingly belted her back, hard. I gasped and began yelling at him. No one standing nearby moved a muscle to help. Rose seemed shocked but not badly hurt. Tim was just becoming aware of what was going on when Tom Webb miraculously rolled up with his car and told us to get in. Believe me, we lost no time.

A few days later the three musketeers were on the road again, this time to the tiny republic of Kirgizstan. Kirgizstan was only about five hours away by bus and although we still had no visas we decided to take the risk. The road wound through dry, windswept steppes for endless miles, with no signs of habitation except an occasional round yurt and a rider minding sheep or cattle. Gradually the snow covered peaks in the distance came closer and our vehicle began to pass through them.

The Tien-Shan mountain range occupies much of the land space of Kirgizstan. During the winter many towns are only accessible by air but the capital, Bishkek, lies in a valley. This is earthquake territory and it isn't unusual for the city to be shaken by a hundred tremors during a year.

To our great surprise it had been arranged for us to

stay with the Campus Crusade students we had met in Moscow. They too seemed pleased at the reunion and it was good to see how well they were fitting into their new environment. Three of the girls were studying Russian, and one was concentrating on Kirgiz. They had already made good friends on campus and were studying the Bible with some of them.

Kirgizstan seemed to fit somewhere in between the other two republics as far as religious freedom was concerned. Evangelism wasn't carried on openly, outside churches, and Christian expatriates came prepared to work as professionals. But churches were growing – most notably those started by Koreans.

Rose and I got the address of one Korean pastor and set off one day to interview him. Within a very short time we were lost. No one we asked seemed to recognise the address. Finally we ran into a smart-looking Russian officer who was in uniform and carrying a briefcase. When he learned I was an American he beamed. 'I love America!' he cried. Slava introduced himself. He was a pilot, teaching at a school for pilots in Bishkek. After listening to our plight he made up his mind to help us and set off down the street with a brisk stride. To our great amusement he also began belting out a hearty rendition of America's national anthem. Slava's English was limited, but that didn't stop him communicating with us. He believed Kirghizstan had big problems and he thought President Yeltsin was no good. But he was sure that one day he would visit America!

After an hour of determined searching, a taxi finally dropped us in front of the pastor's office. Rose and I were overwhelmed at the officer's cheerful kindness in giving up so much of his time. As a gesture of thanks we presented him with a Russian New Testament. With a smile, Slava whipped out two treasures to show us: a small gold cross that he wore around his neck, and a crisp dollar bill. We exchanged addresses and took photos. He kissed our hands and then departed. I have often wondered if our pilot friend ever made it to America.

Pastor and Mrs Chang received us with typical Asian courtesy and hurried to serve us tea. They told us that Bishkek's Korean community numbered about 10,000. Their church had 350 to 400 members but it was attended by a dozen different nationalities. Right now they were renting the city's modern Philharmonic Hall each Sunday – they had even hired a small orchestra to play for them! The Changs had seen a lot of response during their fourteen months in the city. They had baptised two hundred who wanted to follow Jesus Christ, and had established eight other daughter churches outside Bishkek. The pastor and his wife said they were hoping to build a large new mission centre. Negotiations for land, however, had so far been blocked by Muslim activists.

Several workers we talked to said that Muslim activists had also threatened them. Pressure was being exerted on local schools to teach the Koran, but neither students nor teachers were keen on the idea. When the Koran had been translated into the Kirgiz language the previous spring, many people expressed dismay and declared it couldn't possibly be a holy book! The New Testament had also been translated but not well, according to missionaries. Plans for a new edition were underway. 'We work here with a sense of urgency,' we heard them say many times. 'We live with the knowledge that tomorrow, everything could change.'

With only 600,000 residents Bishkek had a smaller, more manageable feel than the other capitals. A walk down the main street led past distinguished government buildings and a modern museum. The Historical Museum had been called the Lenin Museum until recently, and Lenin's statue still dominated the forecourt. I spent hours inside, studying the artwork and exhibits that told the story of the land and its people. The open-air bazaar, however, told us its own story, one similar to what we had seen in the other republics. Ordinary men and women scraped a living any way they could, peddling anything and everything under the sun. Some of the old women had spread used clothing on the ground to sell, or sat with a pathetic heap of apples, or plastic bags – Tim kept buying them, just to give the women a little something.

Once back in Alma-Ata we began preparing for our return to England. Our visas expired on 30 October, our plane tickets were for 3 November. We managed to extend the visas through an agency in Kazakstan, but somehow that wasn't good enough for Moscow. An official stopped us as we were passing through customs at the international airport and declared the extensions were illegal. We had the choice of paying a fine of $110 each or missing our flight back to England. Frustrated though we were, we knew they had us. The system was riddled with bureaucracy, bribery and corruption. Fortunately we had just enough money left between us to pay the fine.

It took time to readjust to life back in England – not so much jet lag as culture lag. I found myself looking with new eyes at the luxuries I had taken for granted. Our colleagues welcomed Tim and I as though we had been to the middle of nowhere and back – but Central Asia was no longer 'nowhere' to us. Nor had its people ever been forgotten by their creator. We had seen the winds of change sweeping the barren steppes of Central Asia, and God himself was riding those storms to bring them hope.

3

The strangers among us

A sharp wind swept across the square, snuffing out the candle I was holding. I shivered. In the darkness it was not difficult to cast my imagination back to a cold night fifty-five years before, when the residents of Mosbach, Germany, stood on these same cobblestones watching a Jewish synagogue torched and burned to the ground. *Vergesst es nicht*. Never forget this night. The words were inscribed on a synagogue memorial tablet nearby. Some pilgrims had planted candles in front of the stone, testifying that they, at least, had not forgotten.

In January 1993 a demonstration in Mosbach and others all over the state of Württemburg were intended to show German solidarity against violence and racism. Earlier in the day I had watched over two thousand students march on the square. 'There comes a time when we need a certain call, when the world must come together as one', the voices of the young people rang with the familiar lyrics of Michael Jackson. 'We are the world, we are the people . . . !' And on a given signal, hundreds of elementary-aged children released white balloons for a dramatic finale.

On the fringes of the crowd a small group of skinheads tried to attract attention. Overwhelmed by numbers, they soon gave up and melted away. I asked various bystanders what they thought of the march. 'It is important that other countries see what we do today,' responded a young teacher, with tears in her eyes. 'But I am ashamed the town had to arrange this. We should have marched before they asked.'

Spontaneous protests had taken place in Germany after the deaths, a few months before, of a Turkish woman and child. The tragedy was a culmination of 1,800 assaults on immigrants, with seventeen deaths, during 1992. Jewish cemeteries had been desecrated, concentration camp memorials set on fire. But although most Germans were appalled by the explosion of neo-Nazi hatred, discontent over the number of immigrants swelling the population was definitely spreading.

This fact was never more shockingly evident than last summer, when 2000 bystanders in Rostock applauded as a mob set fire to a house occupied by asylum-seekers. Soon after, a former SS officer won a Berlin election largely with the slogan, 'No More Foreigners!' 'Those who have been here a long time are welcome,' an older Mosbach resident told me, 'but not the *ausländers* who come to get rich in Germany!' Another man added, 'When the Turks first came we needed them as workers. Now there is unemployment . . .'

After leaving Mosbach I stayed a few days with OM refugee workers Brock and Maren Grigsby in Ludwigsburg. They explained that much of the hostility toward refugees sprang from three popular misconceptions. The first was that the newcomers were taking housing that should go to Germans. In actual fact, 90 per cent of refugees lived in dormitory-style hostels made from old converted warehouses or army barracks, with shared kitchen and bathroom facilities. This kind of housing would be unacceptable to

Germans. Immigrants could not, for the most part, afford ordinary flats. Some landlords insured themselves against an invasion by placing classified newspaper ads that warned, 'Only Germans need apply.'

Other citizens claimed that the refugees were a drain on the economy. In a 1988 to 1991 study, it was proven that a sixteen billion deutschmark (eleven billion dollars) expenditure on refugees was far overbalanced by a fifty-seven billion mark (thirty-eight billion dollars) income realised from refugee employment taxes. In other words, the country made a sizeable profit from immigrants.

The third widely held belief among the German populace was that most refugees were criminals. While there was undeniably an element who abused the system or who engaged in theft, drugs, etc., the Grigsbys maintained that the media's disproportionate coverage of such individual cases gave the vast majority of asylum seekers a negative image.

Following World War Two, Germany offered refuge to any individual fleeing from political, religious or economic persecution. At the time of my visit, the invitation had narrowed to political refugees. Only 4 per cent of all those who arrived in the country ended up receiving permission to stay. Even so, Germany's door was open far wider than any of its European neighbours and half a million applicants were expected in 1993 alone, including thousands of ex-Yugoslavs. To cope with the situation every city and town was required to house 1.25 refugees per 100 citizens. Part of the problem was the ever-increasing backlog in processing applicants. One young Ethiopian in a Stuttgart camp told me he had been waiting over two years for an interview. The practice of refusing language lessons to refugees-in-waiting (except children) further isolated them from the Germans. Up until 1991 they were also barred from employment. Although working was now permissible jobs were scarce, and few skilled foreigners could hope for positions equal to their qualifications.

Economic migrants exacerbated the situation. These men and women arrived in Germany fully aware that they would be refused permanent residence but hoping to milk the system for as long as they could. Often they sent their earnings, as well as clothing or anything else they had, back to families in Africa or Asia or Eastern Europe. And when their time was up, there was always the possibility of running away and starting over in another city, registering under a new name. Abuse of the system had served to rouse the German public's wrath to such an extent that the real anguish of those who had been forcibly torn from their homes and loved ones often went unnoticed. Already traumatised, men and women were wounded further as they suffered rejection. Even Russian Jews, invited to make their homes in Germany and therefore enjoying a more privileged status, ended up disillusioned when they found themselves unable to move from the camps. Suicides occurred all too often.

I wanted to know how God's Church was responding to all of this. It seemed apparent to me that the massive social upheaval also provided an unprecedented opportunity. At few moments in history had so many peoples of the world, of so many faiths, sought shelter under the umbrella of a Christian nation.

As my colleagues and I gave out Christian literature in one of the refugee camps, an East European stopped. He accepted a leaflet and inquired curiously, 'Are you Mormons or Jehovah's Witnesses?' Like the majority of other residents, this man had never seen members of any other denomination visit his dormitory.

Here and there, individuals or Christian fellowships were attempting some form of outreach. The city of Ludwigsburg had three refugee camps housing over a thousand foreigners. Through the encouragement of OM, one church had begun to host an English-speaking international fellowship on Sunday afternoons. Another group paid weekly visits to a rather grim-looking facility that had been a prison, to distribute clothing and to play with the children. But such initiatives were relatively rare. 'Many people feel insecure about approaching foreigners,' explained OM Germany's field leader, Fritz Schuler. 'I believe the Church in general is very interested, they just don't know what to do. That's why we hold workshops. We want to get alongside churches and show them how they can make a difference.'

Training weekends held at the OM base in Mosbach have acquainted Christians with the location of refugee hostels near them and ways to approach strangers with cultural sensitivity. Participants spend most of the time in the camps just making friends. 'There is still a great need for a change in attitude in our country,' observed a worker who had spent five years helping Turkish and Kurdish refugees in the Mosbach area. 'Marches are good, but learning to live every day with foreigners – and incarnating the gospel to them – is more important.'

According to Henk and Irene Wolthaus, who worked with immigrants near Stuttgart, the most enthusiastic witness was provided by the refugees themselves. 'Some of them are real fireballs. They continue in their faith when they leave Germany for other countries. One Vietnamese man we worked with has emigrated to Canada and pulled together a fellowship of 400 other Vietnamese in Edmonton. And the

Lord is also working among Ethiopians in Germany in a unique way. Fellowship groups have doubled and tripled; and they have even translated Bible studies into their own language.'

For the OM team, extending friendship to strangers in a strange land often meant taking them home for an evening or weekend, and allowing them to feel part of the family. It meant providing some special times for the children. It might also include helping asylum-seekers fill out troublesome forms or find the right offices. Many times, the team served most simply by listening.

As I talked with Negra, a teenager who had fled with her family from Bosnia; and heard the story of Victor and Lena, a Russian couple separated from their three-year-old son, I began to understand something of what listening actually meant. Taking time to admire the treasured family photos of an Armenian believer, looking into the ravaged face of Maria, who could not yet speak about the husband and child she had lost in an Indian bomb blast, I realised that neo-Nazis were not the only ones in the wrong. The responsibility for the strangers who live among us – in all our nations – belongs especially to followers of Jesus Christ. For we know what others do not: that Jesus understands the anguish of an immigrant because, for our sake, he had become one himself.

'The Church needs to lead the way,' workers told me. 'This is a historic time . . . and the Lord wants to use this situation to shake us up. If we do not act in the next two or three years, it will be too late.'

4

Go tell it on the mountains!

'A book about God?' The woman extended her workworn hand for the Gospel of John I held, and repeated my stumbling Albanian with a look of dawning wonder. 'A book about God!' She held it up to the view of a curious neighbour, who eagerly advanced for her own copy.

As word spread through the village we were followed from house to house by a gathering troupe of children. We stopped to teach them a simple song and I was reminded that Albania, with a population of three and a quarter million, was the only country in Europe with more children than adults. Almost every household encouraged us to step inside. Most of these remote villagers had never met a foreigner before or read God's love letter to them. But if we had lingered to talk it would not have been possible to reach the next mountain, or the next valley. And if we didn't make it, who would?

I was one of over a hundred international volunteers who had gone to Albania for Easter 1993 to attend the OM Scripture distribution campaign. OM was one of several missions co-operating to reach the whole country. We had just ten days to do our share. In actual fact, I was still catching my breath after a quick trip to Romania. A family called the Todds had asked if I wanted to travel to Romania with them just before the campaign. I jumped at the chance. Romania was a bit out of the way and two days wasn't much time to explore, but it was a lot better than nothing. And they were willing to pay for my visa!

We rendezvoused at the train station in Budapest. Three men who turned out to be deacons from the Oradea Baptist Church in Romania were waiting with a van to drive us the remaining five hours to our destination. At the border we held our breath: a few dozen trucks were lined up ahead of us, awaiting inspection. But we were waved through after a simple passport check and completion of forms – a marked change from the interrogation and searches all would-be visitors could expect just a few years before. Oradea was close to the border and we got into bed about 2 a.m. at a local hotel, thanks to the Todd's generosity. My room even boasted a TV (which didn't work) and hot water (which worked only at certain times), so by Romanian standards it was luxurious.

After the collapse of Ceauşescu's dictatorship, Oradea had begun to benefit right away because of its proximity to Hungary. Young people in the streets were sporting trendy jeans and jogging suits. Shops, while still not crowded with merchandise, were able to display clothes and toiletries imported from Germany and other countries. Mars bars, Snickers and Pepsi had even made their début. The problem was that salaries had not matched inflation. On a monthly average wage of forty-five dollars few could afford to buy the tantalisingly displayed Western products. Grocery stores still looked like something out of the past, stocked with old-fashioned jars and tins. Horse-drawn carts were in common use and those lucky enough to afford cars could expect to queue for petrol. I counted fifty vehicles waiting at one station.

But while life hadn't changed significantly for many Romanians since the Revolution, it was clearly a 'brave new world' for Christians. The first stop on our whirlwind tour was the Oradea Bible Institute, the first school of its kind – apart from a small seminary in Bucharest. The institute offered a four-year, university level programme leading to a Master of Divinity and four other major degrees. The 330 men and women currently enrolled at the institute came from Romania, Moldova, Ukraine, and the former Yugoslavia. 'The need was so great we couldn't not do something,' Dean of Students Radu Gheorghita told me. Classes were being held in a hotel until the institute could build a campus on property it had purchased. A Christian high school was also flourishing. Principal Florin Negrut informed us there were now seven Christian high schools in the country. 'It's a miracle . . . You cannot have Christian education without Christian teachers, and we could find very few from the former USSR. But God kept an element alive.' Negrut should know, he was one of the teachers who lost his job under Communism.

The economic and political uncertainties of the new government were clearly not slowing the 'full steam ahead' mentality of Oradea's believers. When we met with the director of the Romanian Missionary Society's publishing house, Luca Cretan, he enthused: 'We are rebuilding this country! The private sector is being allowed more freedom because everything else has failed. We have to put our foot in now, into publishing, radio and TV.'

We were shown a modern, four-floor publishing and editing facility that would soon be occupied by the Romanian Missionary Society. Next door, a brand new printshop staffed by local Christians was busily turning out thousands of copies of much needed books.

Another stop was a state-of-the-art orphanage built by a Swedish charity. Nothing could have been more of a contrast from the 'chambers of horror' we had come to expect from TV documentaries. The facility's 100 children lived in separate family units, each 'home' with its own caring Christian 'parents'. The comfortable layout, the toys and play equipment were impressive. But not half so impressive as the difference in the children we met. Those who had recently been transferred from other orphanages were easy to spot; malnourished and fearful, they were obviously still working through the physical and mental traumas of their past. But the children who had lived here for some time had blossomed. Their normal play and happy laughter spoke eloquently of the effects of love.

On our last evening we attended a Thursday evening service in the old building that belonged to the Second Baptist Church. A new auditorium was under construction that would seat 3500, but there were already fears it would be too small. Unfortunately we had became lost on the way and by the time we arrived the church was packed out, with scores standing in the back and in the aisles. I was wearing trousers and I knew these Baptists were very conservative: no makeup or jewellery, women on one side and men on the other. I had hoped to slip inconspicuously to the back but to my chagrin we were ushered to the front row, reserved for guests.

What a privilege it was to meet Dr Joseph Ton, the church's first pastor, who happened to be speaking that night. Probably this man more than any other became a major spokesperson for Romanian Christians during his years of banishment to the West. Thanks to Ton's tireless efforts, believers all over the world got involved in rebuilding the country after the Revolution. After the service we stopped for refreshments in the home of a deacon from the church, and then he drove us the long way back to Budapest. By the time our unheated van reached the airport at 2.30 a.m. on 2 April, I was frozen to my seat. Unfortunately the airport was still closed, so we were obliged to sit outside for another two hours. By 7.30 a.m., however, we were in the air and I was too excited to feel my exhaustion. Very soon we would be setting foot in 'the land that time forgot.'

Bordered by the former Yugoslavia in the North and Greece in the South, Albania was the last of the Communist dominoes to fall. So thoroughly did Enver Hoxha and his Communist regime isolate his country from 'contamination' by the outside world that until 1990, no foreign films or newspapers – and especially no religious books – were allowed to cross the borders. Outsiders wishing to visit were often required to have their hair cut, beards shaved, or clothes exchanged for less fashionable attire. And of course, conversation between Albanians and aliens was strictly forbidden.

It was 1993 and Albania's people were gradually awakening to the twentieth century. Most who had once regarded Hoxha as their saviour now hated him – except, perhaps, those who dwelt in the mountains, who were grateful that he had brought them electricity, despite ignoring their need for heat and running water.

After landing in Tirana we found a couple of ramshackle buses waiting to convey us to Durres, the port city OM used as its base. The first thing to hit me as we drove along was the spectacular, raw beauty of the countryside. Snow-mantled mountains formed a backdrop for shepherds tending their flocks and whitewashed stone cottages . . . scenes that might have belonged to a hundred years ago. 'The Land Where Eagles Fly', was the name Albanians themselves gave their country. But picturesque though it was, even a short ride was enough to reveal some of the nation's scars.

For mile after mile we saw stumps in place of trees, the wood sacrificed to keep families from freezing during harsh winters. Schools, like homes, often went unheated, lacking even window panes to keep out the cold breezes. Most startling were the ugly concrete pillboxes that desecrated the land everywhere we looked. Hoxha had convinced his people that the 800,000 bunkers he had built in the fields and front yards of homes would save them when the USA carried out their evil invasion plans. Fence posts topped by steel spikes, like bayonets, were designed to provide an additional welcome to enemy parachutists.

In the afternoon of our first day two OM vans arrived with medical aid which they had just transported a thousand kilometres from Vienna. The supplies were from World Vision and were bound for an obstetrics hospital in Berat. I hadn't slept since arriving from Romania and I was hoping for an early night, but when I was asked to go along and take photographs it was too good an opportunity to miss. We arrived in Berat after nightfall. The doctors and nurses on duty had no warning of our arrival, but they gladly dropped everything to help us unload. Medicines, bandages, baby cream and clothing, steriliser and washing machine – every item brought exclamations of joy. But the *pièce de résistance* was the delivery table. The staff gathered around the modern chrome equipment with an expression near to reverence. Later the director and head of surgery showed us the rusty, archaic tables they were using, and we were able to understand their reaction. Women gave birth to

2600 babies in this 100-bed hospital each year. Now, for some of them at least, the experience would be less of an ordeal.

We stayed overnight in Berat and awoke the next morning to driving rain that turned streets into rivers and paths into a muddy morass. My hostess, Swiss OMer Ruth Geiger, was undeterred. This was her day to visit a local hospital for mentally handicapped children and if we wished to, we could go along.

Ruth tried to prepare us on the way for what we would encounter but it didn't do any good. When we stepped into the derelict building half an hour later I was fighting an immediate urge to be sick. The stench of latrines and unwashed bodies was overpowering. In a bleak-looking dayroom, a row of raggedly clad children sat lethargically on a bench. Several were striking their heads against the crumbling walls. Nobody intervened. Indeed, no one in authority seemed to be around. We found out later that most of the staff were clustered in the building's only heated room. A few boys ran up and clung to me. One of them kissed my hand.

We found the smallest children lying in rusted beds. The rooms were too cold for these four and five-year-olds to emerge from their blankets. When I picked up the chilled little hands, some of the thin faces smiled up at me, while other children flinched from my touch, as though they anticipated abuse. It was clear that not all of the fifty children were mentally deficient. A deaf and dumb boy with a bright, intelligent face learned that I was American and rushed away. He returned a moment later, proudly exhibiting his worn 'America' sweatshirt.

Ruth introduced me to an eighteen-year-old girl born with severe physical deformities. Her dark eyes smiled at me. There was nothing wrong with this young woman's mind, Ruth told me. Yet she was condemned to the prison of her bed for all of her days, with no way of escape. Not even through the pages of a book, for no one had ever taken the trouble to teach her how to read. As we left the hospital a child came to the door, his little voice following us down the muddy path. 'Hello!' he piped hopefully in English, willing us to come back. 'Hello!' My heart broke. Who, I wondered, would bring an end to these children's waking nightmare?

Not long after my visit, a TV crew arrived in Berat and exposed the horror of this children's hospital to the world. Ruth wrote to tell me that the building was forced to close. The children were distributed to other facilities. Whether or not they were any better off, I would never know.

I returned to Durres and spent the next day in orientation. This was mostly a short course in how not to offend the local people. Take your shoes off at the door, we were advised. Drink and eat everything you're served (except for *raki*, the potent local homebrew, which could deck you!). Don't compliment anyone on any object you see in a house or it will be presented to you as a gift. Women should converse only with women, men with men. Expect women to greet you with two to four kisses on both cheeks.

Albanian had to be one of the toughest languages I'd ever come across. In some cases there were as many as 124 ways to pronounce a single word! Even a simple yes and no (*po* and *jo*) could lead to confusion, especially since the accompanying head motions were exactly the opposite to those we use in the West!

We had all heard that Albania was the poorest of European nations. Nevertheless, seeing the evidence was like the difference between black and white. At the time of my visit the average person earned approximately twenty pounds or thirty dollars per month. Forty per cent of the population were jobless. Yet wherever we went, Albanians pressed on us gifts of flowers, eggs, sweets, cups of tea and the inevitable doses of *raki*.

'You may lose everything you own in Albania, but you won't lose weight,' joked a friend. As foreigners we never lacked food, but theft was a constant headache. One of our campaign vehicles turned up the first morning without a front grill, indicator lights and mirror. Later our Berat van lost a headlight and very nearly its windscreen wipers too when a boy climbed on the hood and brazenly attempted their removal right in front of us! Anthea from New Zealand returned to the village home where she was staying and discovered three men going through her belongings. But the surprise was on them. The small bottle they uncapped wasn't perfume, but tear gas! Anthea had equipped herself with the device after an assault the previous year.

The Albanian homes I shared and most that I visited had only two small rooms. One family numbered eleven members, ranging in age from newborn to grandmother! Yet their homes were kept scrupulously tidy, and each visitor was welcomed with delight. Families that could afford black and white TVs seemed to keep them on non-stop, even during meals. Perhaps it was an attempt to make up for all of the years when they knew nothing of the outside world. The toilet was usually the Turkish type, a porcelain hole in the floor, and it was flushed with scoops of water. We had been admonished not to clog the system by throwing paper down the pipes. When someone summoned the courage to ask what we should do with it, however, he got no answer. Most horrifying was the discovery that in most homes the toilet space doubled as the kitchen! Aside from the unhygienic implications, the arrangement made for nonstop traffic jams. And bathing was a major undertaking – water had to be heated for bucket baths on the same two-ring kerosene stove that was used for preparing the meals – while some of the houses in the cities were able to boast cold water showers.

Our Easter outreach concentrated on distributing to towns and rural villages Gospels of John and New Testaments. The whole Albanian Bible would not be available for several more months. My own team was assigned to cover the area surrounding Berat. Each day as our van left this mountain city we could look up at the giant letters cut into the stone slope high above us: 'ENVER'. Although Enver Hoxha, the dictator who had strangled the soul of this country for forty-one years was now dead, the enduring presence of his name mocked us still.

Ours was a most unique invasion. We took our van to places where horses, donkeys and the backs of men and women were the common burden carriers. We saw people farming with the crudest of implements. Occasionally our vehicle was forced to ford a shallow river at the end of a dirt track. More than once we got out and pushed. But children and adults alike flocked around for open air programmes, and except for the time a translator was bitten by a dog, the reception was always friendly. Even Muslims readily accepted our literature.

The fact was, few Albanians remembered the faith of their fathers. Communism took over in 1945 and the government shut down all places of worship in 1967. Albania was declared the world's first atheistic state. Those who dissented were killed or imprisoned. Now, it seemed, the people were hungry to re-learn what they had been taught to forget. When I presented one seventy-eight-year-old woman with a New Testament her face lit with joy. She kissed me and brought me into her house to show me her dearest treasure, a picture of Jesus. Interest was so great in some villages that OM started three new Bible study groups after the campaign.

The most physically demanding job was trekking to mountain homes that were inaccessible by road. The seven men and women who volunteered for this assignment later told us that these poorest of people sometimes slaughtered a sheep in their honour. The hardest part to swallow was the cooked head they were expected to eat – eyes and all!

'We were watched all the time, even when we tried to use a stream to wash in. But it was so exciting to take the good news to those remote places,' American wife and mother Mary McAllister reported, shaking her head in amazement. 'We asked in one village if they knew Jesus Christ. A lady thought a while and replied, 'I've heard that name somewhere.'

It was apparent to us all that the spiritual and physical wounds of this emerging country ran deep. Recovery would take massive amounts of aid, plus a total rebuilding of the infrastructure. But healing of the spirit also needed to take place. I remembered the day I had watched an Albanian team-mate hold a village child in her arms. Noticing how cold its small bare feet were and believing herself unobserved, Buqe sat down and removed her own shoes and socks. Then she drew the wool onto the feet of the little one. The tender gesture moved me profoundly. And it filled me with hope. For it demonstrated that God's love could make a difference to this 'land where eagles fly'. Through his children the healing of a nation had already begun.

5

Talking Turkey

Why me? I groaned silently as a Heathrow official singled me out of the queue for a security check. My companions looked sympathetic as my carefully packed bag was torn apart and the contents stuffed untidily back. The fact that I wasn't travelling alone on this trip was a comfort. Photographer Tim Wright and his wife Linda had both lived and worked in Turkey before, and their experience would be invaluable in getting around the country. THY Airlines might stand for They Hate You, as Tim suggested, but they delivered us to Istanbul right on schedule at 6 p.m., as dusk was falling.

To understand Istanbul you have to know that it is a city cut in two. The older side is in Europe and is separated from the Asian side by the Sea of Marmara and Bosporus, so most people are obliged to do a lot of commuting. Tim, Linda and I took a catamaran over to the Asian side and there I got my first glimpse of the city skyline. Although shrouded in mist, a few needle-thin minarets stabbing through the clouds reminded me that I was in a place like no other.

Byzantium, Constantinople, Istanbul ... This capital that bridges East and West can take you on a magic carpet-ride through 3000 years of history. More and more tourists come to Turkey to do just that. Or else they make the sunny Mediterranean coast their destination for winter getaways. But the purpose of our visit was far more serious. Turkey was notorious for its long record of human rights violation, and the failure to honour individual freedom of worship was top of the list. The secular constitution was supposed to guarantee freedom of religion. In practice, anyone who openly gave out non-Muslim literature could expect immediate arrest and face jail or deportation.

The couple that Tim, Linda and I were staying with in Istanbul were expert witnesses. Dave Wilson was director of a Bible correspondence course outreach and had been arrested about seven times during his thirteen years in the country. He and his wife Pam had also been imprisoned and deported without a hearing on a number of occasions. We looked through a scrapbook of newspaper clippings that recorded a long history of harrassment, both of Christian workers and local believers.

'Most people on the street, including the police, don't think the dissemination of Christian information is legal,' Dave explained over the next days. 'But it is. The law has always been in place. The important word now is *legitimisation* rather than *legalisation*.' He told us that lawyers had advised them to allow themselves to be arrested, again and again, in order to prove the law. Each time they were acquitted they would be establishing a precedent for freedom. Which all sounds very well, until you realise what it's like to get arrested in Turkey. Pam remembered one particular occasion when she was sentenced to nine days in jail after distributing a Christian leaflet that explained who Jesus was. The police clustered around and ogled her as she was fingerprinted and photographed. One man, unaware that she could understand Turkish, called her a Romanian prostitute. Then Pam was locked in a small, box-like metal cell with only a slit in the door for light. That was the hardest part, because Pam suffers from severe claustrophobia. For the first half of the night she was overcome by episodes of fainting and vomiting. Finally even her guard took pity on her and let her sit in his office. Pam and Dave were both eventually deported, but as on previous occasions they soon returned.

Another time when Dave suddenly disappeared the police denied knowing his whereabouts. Pam frantically began checking hospitals and even the morgue. Finally, the authorities admitted they had taken him into custody. During a ten-month period one year the couple were forced to move every few weeks in order to keep ahead of the police. I began to understand why one of Pam's favourite proverbs was, 'Visit a Turkish bath and you'll sweat!' She and Dave had made up their minds to take whatever came with their commitment, no matter how difficult it was.

When the three of us walked into the Bible correspondence course office on our first morning we discovered a hive of activity. A team of a dozen men and women from Canada and South Africa, Korea, Germany and the USA were hard at work folding, stamping and stuffing envelopes. We were promptly enlisted to give a hand. This small and innocuous-looking office was a spiritual powerhouse. Through its thirty-plus years of operation the correspondence course ministry had resulted in half of the current believers in Turkey.

'Who is Jesus? Have you ever read the New Testament?' ran the advertisements in leading newspapers. 'For more information on the historical life and teachings of Jesus, write to us.' The previous year over ten thousand Turks had responded – the highest number ever. And some of the individuals who received their copies of Scripture wrote back: 'I have not stopped reading the New Testament that you sent me. I read it through the night and have almost finished it. My life will be following a different track from now on.' And another wrote: 'I have read many passages of Scripture to people in my village, often many of them assemble in my house. Before I read, I tell them that they may not agree with it, but that it is very important and that it has changed my life.'

Of course, the office received some hate mail as well. Occasionally Dave and others on the team walked into a trap and found the police waiting to arrest them. Postal workers have been known to destroy course material. Dave had fought – and won – a case against Post Offices which refused to send envelopes stamped with the course's return address. Still, books were hand-delivered whenever possible, and course workers also followed up each contact through letters or personal visits. The goal was to encourage individuals to join indigenous Turkish fellowships wherever they existed, and to plant churches where they didn't. 'The course acts as a filtering system,' Dave told us. 'Some do six or ten courses and don't become believers. Some complete only one and believe. But most say: "I never realised Jesus was like this!" It changes their minds.'

Istanbul was the kind of city where the ancient and the modern sometimes collided incongruously, like a black-veiled woman wearing red stiletto shoes. More and more concrete apartment buildings were being sandwiched between mosques, grace and beauty sacrificed to the demand for accommodation. Morality was clearly on a downward spiral. It was hard to avoid the pornography flaunted in the news-stands and illustrated outside movie theatres and nightclubs. Prostitution was not only legal, but there were state-owned brothels. Abortion was an acceptable option.

I was grateful to my Creator for dark hair and eyes that made me less conspicuous in this country. I remembered my Finnish friend who had struggled working in Turkey a few years before. After the first year she wrote: 'My flatmate is out and I really need someone to talk to. Anyway, life in Turkey is different for her. Her eyes are black. All blue-eyed women are prostitutes. Every child knows that! And if they are single, that confirms it. What other reason would they have to come here? Today a colleague of mine at the secular school where I teach jokingly made a comment about me welcoming any man into my bed. I couldn't say a word back, but tears accompanied me all the way home. Five times I've been spat at in the face, and I was just waiting for the bus. What happens in the bus itself is another story. For four months I've been trying to get a residence permit but nothing is working out. Nobody takes you seriously. You are just a little prostitute, so who cares? Ultimately, of course, what counts is what the Lord has in mind. But I guess my make-up is such that after swallowing the hurt, I start cracking up. I love Turkey. But I don't know if I can live here.' My friend ended up going home.

From Istanbul the three of us took an overnight trip to visit workers in Bursa, a few hours away. This was my first bus ride through the spring countryside and I might have enjoyed it, except for the fact that all Turkish men seem to be dedicated to acquiring lung cancer. The cigarettes they smoked were particularly vile-smelling. To make it worse, Turks dislike breezes and won't open windows. Opening ours earned the same dirty looks as we would have received if we had blown our noses in public.

Ken and Trudi were Americans from Silicon Valley, California. They told us that when they first arrived two years before, they had found only one Christian in a city of one million people. Now there were seven. 'We really wanted to do church planting in an area of Turkey where no one else was,' they explained. I thought they'd picked a good place, as Bursa was a conservative Muslim stronghold. Another family who had gone there in the 1980s had made little progress before they were deported and a second couple gave up after only a year.

Ken and Trudi had been through some tough times themselves. Two men had infiltrated their Bible study group the previous spring, and leaked names and phone numbers to a radical Islamic group. But after two months of threatening telephone calls, the harrassment mysteriously stopped. 'It's only been these last few months that things have really started happening,' Ken declared enthusiastically. 'The most exciting development is a seeker's group. The Lord has been doing so much lately I almost hate to go to sleep! I don't want to miss anything.'

The couple's two little girls were natural charmers who made friends easily with neighbours in their apartment block. Other women were amazed at the control Trudi had over their three-year-old. 'Lydia actually does what she's told! In this society children often misbehave. Either they're given no discipline at all or they're beaten.' Trudi added, 'Turkish people can really sense what kind of person you are. We never argue with them about Islam. We just talk about Jesus. And we show people we care about them.'

After returning to Istanbul we decided to save time and catch a domestic flight to the city of Diyarbakir, on the other side of the country. Diyarbakir was like a frontier town straight out of the Wild West – only this was the Wild East version. Shaggy, fierce-looking men crowded the badly rutted streets. The women were either shrouded head-to-toe in black, or wearing colourful Kurdish headscarves and dresses. One desperate mother sat begging, holding a sleeping child who was probably drugged. Horse-drawn wagons and other vehicles stirred up clouds of dust. Only the guns were missing, or at least kept out of sight. The city was under martial law.

Diyarbakir, Turkey, is described in guidebooks as 'an ancient walled city on the Tigris River.' Standing on top of the thick walls I was thrilled by my first glimpse of the Fertile Crescent, which I had been taught was the cradle of civilisation. But Diyarbakir wasn't exactly the kind of place you would normally choose to settle in and bring up your kids. The city was a hotbed of rebellion. Eighty-five per cent of its residents were Kurds, whose identity as a separate people the Turkish government refused to acknowledge. Until a few years before, it was even forbidden to use the word 'Kurd'. Kurds were 'mountain Turks'. They could not wear their own dress, speak their own language, or teach their children Kurdish customs. Although these repressive measures had eased a little, the tension between Turks and Kurds in eastern Turkey was still explosive. And Diyarbakir was the flashpoint.

But to Canadians Clarke and Nancy Gourlay, Diyarbakir was home. The couple had met five years before in Montreal, where Clarke was taking a degree in Middle East studies. After their marriage and having gained some experience working among Iranian immigrants, they moved to Turkey. By early 1991 they had already learnt much of the language and were ready to start planting churches. But then the Gulf War broke out. Saddam Hussein, thwarted in his efforts to annex Kuwait, turned his forces against the Kurds of northern Iraq. While the world watched in horror men, women and children fled to the mountains. Thousands died. Finally galvanised into action, the UN began setting up refugee camps, airlifting food and medicine.

Clarke and Nancy were among the Christian workers in Turkey who responded to the crisis. For five exhausting weeks they worked alongside other volunteers in the camps of northern Iraq. 'As a group we set up and staffed two hospitals, ran kids' clubs, built outhouses, distributed tents, blankets, medicine and food, buried people, shared the gospel, prayed with people.' The experience was bound to have a deep effect. When, the following September, they travelled back to the east of Turkey and saw the suffering that remained among the Kurds, they knew they had to act. In October 1991 the couple moved to Diyarbakir which was about four hours from the Iraq border and a centre for the distribution of aid. Two months later their first child was born.

For the short time we stayed with the Gourlays I shared a room with their German co-worker, Ursula. Ursula had also been among the volunteers in a Kurdish camp, helping over one hundred thousand refugees. 'We started a tent hospital,' she remembered, 'and I assisted there for about three weeks, until I became unwell. I think it was mostly exhaustion – I weighed only forty-six kilos at the time.'

Ursula spent some time recuperating and when she returned to Turkey she heard of the need for UNHCR staff. Ursula then moved back to the Turkish-Iraq border and for eight hours a day over the next three months, listened to countless horror stories from the refugees. It was a heart-rending job. Often she found herself weeping with the people she interviewed. Eventually some Muslims obtained literature from the Christian staff and told that UN authorities they were being proselytised against their will. Although it was a set-up, Operation Mercy workers were forced to withdraw to Diyarbakir.

Clarke and Nancy now provided local direction for an international relief and development agency. They were also part of a church planting team. A Bible study group was meeting regularly and several Kurdish believers had taken a bold stand, accepting baptism and witnessing openly to friends. The Gourlays admitted that life in Diyarbakir had its share of challenges. Snow that year had lasted from November through to April, and their house had no central heating. One morning Nancy found a cup of water beside her bed frozen solid. And when the temperature dropped to minus 25°C all the water pipes burst. In summer the temperatures soared the other way, up to a sizzling 47°C.

In spite of the discomforts Nancy insisted that she liked the place. Even their little son had taken to Turkey – his favourite breakfast was white cheese, olives and sweet tea! They rented a house with enough land for little Raymond to play on, and had proudly grown what was probably the only lawn in Diyarbakir. Nancy loved gardening, although it could be discouraging. She showed me two stunted rose-bushes that she had patiently replanted after neighbourhood children had pulled them up. Somehow the bushes seemed to symbolise the Gourlays' efforts to establish the hope of Jesus Christ in this hostile soil, which required planting and replanting, again and again.

Nancy enjoyed a good relationship with the local women. For Ursula, single in a society that valued the female sex according to how many children they had, the situation was a lot more frustrating. 'They treat me like I'm a fourteen-year-old because I have no children,' she sighed. 'Some try to find me a nice Muslim to marry! They have a lot of prejudices against Westerners and Christians.' I asked Ursula how she was able to keep going. She smiled. 'Because I believe God will bring salvation to the Kurds – and I want to be here when it happens! They have suffered so much. The cross is a symbol of torture even here, and I think the cross is the only thing that will help the Kurds understand, and restore them. My only wish is that God will reach them through me.'

The roar of jet fighters and helicopters flying low over the house often drowned out our conversations. Newspaper headlines carried constant news of bombings, terrorist attacks, kidnappings, protests and uprisings. Once the Gourlays were in the town centre when someone nearby was shot through the back of the head. In the ensuing fight between police and murderer a bullet went through their car window. But they stayed on, as Ursula did, because they knew they were where God wanted them to be – and because they had chosen to translate their faith into practical action. 'There are people in this world struggling every day for existence,' said Clarke. 'The West needs to realise that and do something about it.'

After a few days Tim, Linda and I boarded a bus in Diyarbakir and headed for Iraq. The windows didn't open and everyone on board chain-smoked the whole four and a half hours. By the end of the trip my head was a ticking bomb, my stomach was heaving, and I had broken into a cold sweat. Fortunately, two OMers were waiting to escort us over the border. I had the distinct feeling we would need our wits about us for what lay ahead.

6

'We who face death'

The sign 'Welcome to Kurdistan' greeted us as we rolled over the Turkish border into northern Iraq. We were now in a never-never land that didn't exist on anyone's world map and probably never would. It was late spring, and I admired the green-velvet countryside which would soon be scorched brown under 46°C heat. It was hard to envisage that the Kurds we passed in the fields and sleeping villages were the target for annihilation by Saddam Hussein, just two years before.

Four thousand bombed villages and 80,000 deaths later, Iraq's three million surviving Kurds dwelt within a 'safe haven' protected by the UN. But how safe was it? On our way we had heard rumours of a UN withdrawal. The inhabitants of Kurdistan were well aware that if their protectors left, the cobra next door was poised to strike. Saddam Hussein had lost none of his venom. His government had in fact offered a $20,000 bounty on the lives of all foreigners in Kurdistan with the aim of sabotaging relief efforts. It was a strange feeling to know that Tim, Linda and I had a price on our heads – I'd probably never been worth so much before in my life. To balance things a little, the Kurdistan government ruled that anyone caught causing trouble to an NGO (non-government officer) could expect the death sentence. Nobody even dared to complain if an aid vehicle was parked in the wrong place.

We were staying at the Shelter Now International (SNI) base as guests of a South African couple, Julian and Peni Davison. The Davisons had originally been commissioned for service in Turkey by Archbishop Desmond Tutu, back in 1991. Eight months into language study they were asked to drive a vehicle from Turkey and deliver it to relief workers in northern Iraq. The five days Peni and Julian spent in the war-torn zone opened their eyes. Soon after their return to Turkey, the director of SNI in Iraq sent a plea to the couple's field leader: 'Send them back!' The mission agreed for the Davisons to be seconded to SNI, and they took over as directors in 1992. Peni and Julian described the staggering challenge that faced them. The Iraqi army invasion had left thousands of Kurds homeless, living in tents and makeshift shelters, and winter was approaching fast.

'We felt so helpless! SNI needed to provide 2,500 homes for displaced families before the onset of bad weather. Everything was against us: the lack of materials, finances, manpower and transport; our inability to speak the language; adjustment to a different culture; and most important – time! The Kurds would not have to fear Saddam Hussein if the winter returned before shelters were complete. They would starve and freeze to death.' As Julian co-ordinated the overall activities of SNI, Peni undertook responsibility as building project manager. Under her was a staff of 120 Muslim men – an unheard-of position of authority for a woman in that part of the world. But somehow Peni made it work. By the spring of 1993 SNI had completed 7,000 houses capable of housing 70,000 Kurds.

The Davisons offered to show us some of them. As we

left the valley for the mountains Julian pointed out the widespread erosion caused by the felling of trees for fuel. In many places land slides or runoff from the rain and snow had washed out the road. We skirted around a huge boulder and then a crater gouged out by a bomb. Julian stopped to allow us to take photos. He warned us, however, not to stray into the innocent-looking fields spattered with red poppies and dandelions. The area had probably been mined.

Our two Toyota Land Cruisers remained in close two-way radio contact. 'This is a PKK area,' Julian explained. The PKK – Kurdistan Workers' Party – were a guerrilla force determined to carve an independent Kurdistan from Turkey. As their terrorist methods had made them less than popular in Turkey, they now hid in the bordering mountains. Occasionally they came into conflict with the Iraqi Kurdish militia who were called, rather significantly, *pesh merga* – 'We Who Face Death.' Ahead we ran into a blockade of *pesh merga* heavily armed with AK-47s and grenades. They had news that members of the PKK were in the vicinity and insisted that we take along two guards for protection. The men climbed into the back of our vehicle with their Kalashnikovs ready for business.

Arriving at the destroyed Kurdish village where we planned to eat lunch we found a dozen more men from the militia. PKK forces were just over the hill, they told us urgently. We had to get out at once. While the soldiers consulted I wandered away. I had spotted a group of men moving sheep over the next ridge and wanted to get a closer shot with my camera. I met Tim halfway back. 'What on earth were you doing?' he demanded. 'Do you know who you were taking a picture of? PKK! They could have grabbed you!' I knew that for once, Tim wasn't joking. More than one foreigner had vanished in this no man's land, and I could have been held for ransom or even killed. We left without further ado.

Back in the valley we stopped in a village to inspect the foundations of a new school. This was only one of eighty Kurdish villages rebuilt under the auspices of SNI. The houses were primitive by Western standards, two or three rooms made of mud bricks, but far more substantial than the shelters they had replaced. SNI was now in the process of erecting schools – one for every two or three villages. The idea was to encourage Kurds to live in the country where they could farm the land and become self-supporting, rather than stay in cities where they were only consumers. About 70 per cent of families who originally fled their homes to escape Saddam's army had returned.

Wherever our SNI vehicles went we were hailed with smiles and waves. It was clear how much Julian and Peni meant to the Kurds. It was also clear that they had grown to love these people as their own. 'There's no pretence here that things are OK,' said Peni. 'I find a greater degree of honesty among the Kurds than among my own people in South Africa, and they are more receptive because of that. They observe everything you do. So it's important that they see the joy of the Lord.'

They related an extraordinary tale about a Kurdish architect, Ali, who had accompanied Peni to a distant village building site. Just as they reached the village, their Land Cruiser ran out of petrol. There wasn't a drop anywhere to be had. When Peni and Ali finished their business they climbed back into the vehicle. Peni prayed while Ali turned the key in the ignition, and the engine fired. The jeep took them all the way back to the base in Zakho. The architect was thunderstruck. 'I believe! I believe!' he declared, unable to refute the evidence of Peni's faith in God. Ali and his wife had begun to meet regularly with the Davisons for Bible study and discipleship, along with others. Kurds had been abused and murdered by fellow Muslims. The love of Christians, delivered to them in such practical ways, was not something they could ignore. When another group visited and stated openly that they were missionaries, the Kurdistan government's response was unexpected: 'You are most welcome! Bring as many friends as you can.'

Now that the majority of houses and schools were completed, Peni and Julian were anxious to begin another SNI project. In just one area they'd surveyed in Zakho they had discovered the existence of 1500 Kurdish widows, most living in desperate conditions. 'They are the leftovers,' said Peni, 'that relief agencies haven't helped.'

She described how they had gone from door to door and come upon a dark, cave-like dwelling with no light at all. 'I waded through water and felt with my hands. And there, in the corner, was a pallet with a little old lady on it. She had no food, and nothing but a rag covering her. I asked her, "Who is feeding you?" She told me another widow who had eight children baked bread and sold it. If there was enough food, they gave her some. "There is no one for me," she kept saying. "There is no one for me!"' Peni's face mirrored her distress. 'I just wanted to hold her and cry.' The Davisons planned to re-settle the neediest women and children in better shelters and provide projects for self-support. 'It's important for the community to see them as contributors, not just consumers . . . So many of the women feel forgotten,' Peni added. 'They need people to show they care about them. And they need to find their worth in God.'

Some staff members were soon functioning under the name of Operation Mercy, a relief wing of OM born during the Kurdish crisis two years before. Along with the widows' project they were hoping to make pre-natal care available. A nurse from Nebraska, USA, had arrived in Iraq the previous September planning to spend only a few months. But after being exposed to the medical work in the Kurdish villages, Joan made up her mind to stay. 'So many of the things we saw could have been prevented with simple hygiene,' she told me. 'I began to get a burden for health education . . . I also wanted Muslim women to know that God loved them. Health care is a means of removing the spiritual veil from their lives. I really believe that with Jesus, their lives will be different.' We stopped in the Zakho hospital to see twenty-two-year-old Barb, another American who volunteered as a nurse's aid. 'My first morning here I saw a man with his leg blown off from a mine. My head spun. I thought, Lord, what am I doing here? But the patients can see the difference if you care. I know this is where God wants me.' Tim was able to photograph Barb taking care of a young Kurdish girl – another innocent mine victim. Months, even years after the invasion, Saddam was still claiming lives.

As we left the hospital our driver was already ahead of us, checking the Toyota's undercarriage for explosives. Vehicles at the SNI base, like the office itself, were protected twenty-four hours a day by armed guards. Yet caution was always necessary. On New Year's Eve a bomb was planted in the office's garden wall. By God's grace the blast caused only structural damage. 'We were actually planning to meet there that night for prayer and fellowship,' commented Malaysian staff member Thye Soo. 'Just two hours before the party we changed to another house instead.' Thye Soo seemed to take such incidents in his stride; he grinned good-naturedly when co-workers teased him about the time he'd gone mountain-climbing with friends. When a bullet hit a nearby rock they all panicked and scrambled for cover. But the rifleman proved friendly – he only wanted to warn the men they were walking into a mined area. Thye Soo had worked eleven years in a bank before responding to God's call to serve in another land. He was now handling SNI finances as well as assisting other relief organisations that needed computer help. 'I'm like a big fish in a small pond,' he laughed. 'Nobody over here knows about computers!'

But Thye Soo had also faced some dark moments. He confided the shock it had been, one time, to enter a village after it had been bombed and find what was left of the men, women and children. 'You learn to hate war,' he said quietly. 'Coming here is the Master's course in reality.'

The tension of living so close to a battle zone inevitably took its toll. So did the less dramatic hardships – contending with the suffocating summer heat and flies, the treacherous roads and constant power cuts, and the loneliness of being cut off from the outside world.

I was told UN guards in Kurdistan received high risk pay of $200 per day. Professional UNICEF and UN staff reportedly started with a salary of $9000 per month. Peni and Julian lived on donations of about $200 a month and the single workers half that amount. Yet they were content. 'We have so many opportunities to share because of what we're doing,' they insisted. Only the Christmas before, the staff had acted out a nativity play that was broadcast on TV, with a potential five hundred thousand viewers. Some Christians, Julian observed, have trouble accepting mercy ministries as a legitimate part of the great commission. They think of such work as a 'cover' for real ministry. This attitude disturbed Julian. He emphasised that meeting spiritual and physical needs went hand in hand: 'Relief is not a cover for ministry, but ministry in itself. It speaks loudly of what a Christian is.'

Peni and Julian looked tired. The demands on them were enormous, and, safe haven or not, the Kurds of Iraq would need help for a long time to come. In the final analysis, they knew, the only truly safe haven was the Lord Jesus himself. And the privilege of proclaiming him only belonged to those who earned the right.

The ride from Iraq was twice as long, but not half as bad as the journey in. Our bus was a brand new double-decker boasting the unheard-of luxury of a no-smoking section. We paused in Gazientep, Turkey, long enough to interview a pair of Christian workers in the city, then travelled on to Adana. Andrew and Debbie had been in Turkey's cotton and citrus capital for about seven years, although both had lived in the country longer than that. 'Adana was the last place I wanted to come,' admitted Andrew, a quietly-spoken Oxford graduate. 'Anarchy was at its peak in 1979. There were bombs and shootings in Adana and the whole climate was fear. Only four months before, another worker had been killed in his home. I was unmarried then, sent to replace a man who was told by police he was next on the hit list. To be honest, I was scared!' But Andrew moved anyway and found a position teaching at a language school. Later he became an English instructor at the university. In 1982 the small team received a blow when Joop Hoogteyling of Holland, father of two, died inexplicably of heart failure. Three years later the authorities launched a major crackdown on Christians in the area. Andrew was arrested at the university, but although others were deported, he was somehow spared.

Andrew met Debbie at an OM conference and they were married in 1986. The Adana team had shrunk to only one other couple by that time. Debbie was still learning

Turkish when their team-mates were deported. Adana was proving to be spiritually resistant territory. 'Most of my colleagues are embarrassed to talk about religion, including Islam,' remarked Andrew. 'But they are very superstitious: fortune-telling and consulting clairvoyants is very common. And although many won't touch pork, almost every grocer sells spirits and alcohol, which is also forbidden by Islam.' Debbie and Andrew and their two little children lived almost next door to a mosque – not an unusual situation in Turkey, where mosques mushroom on every corner. They probably didn't even hear the pre-dawn call to prayer that jolted me out of bed, but they looked drained. The past year had been particularly discouraging, they said. The real battle in Turkey was not so much for people to come to the Lord, but for believers who would go on with him.

Before we left Adana, we asked Andrew to take us to the cemetery where the American David Goodman was buried. As I stood before the simple gravestone I felt profoundly moved. A dozen years had passed since that June morning when David had opened his front door, and fallen victim of a random extremist killing. I thought of his wife, Jenny, expecting their first child at the time. And I remembered the scrap of paper that had been found in David's pocket, with the words: 'Be strong and courageous. Do not be afraid or discouraged . . . for there is a greater power with us than with him' (2 Chr 32:7).

David and Jenny Goodman, the Wilsons, Andrew and Debbie . . . so many had paid and were still paying the price to win back this land. It was here that Christ's followers had first been called Christians. It was here that the first churches had taken root. How long before Turkey returned to its first love?

Back in Istanbul we used our last few days to explore

and take photos. The famous old covered bazaar lured us, its maze of arched passageways crammed with carpets, hand-decorated plates and tiles, hookahs, jewellery – and tenacious venders. Topkapi Palace is the most popular of the tourist attractions, and with good reason. While the exterior is not so impressive, the fairy-tale wealth of the sultans displayed inside took my breath away. Among the jewels in the treasury were daggers fashioned of emeralds and diamonds, thrones of ivory, even robes that still bore the bloodstains caused by assasins. The bones reputed to belong to the wrist and skull of John the Baptist, a genuine footprint of the prophet Mohammad, plus a few hairs from his beard were all displayed to amaze and inspire the visitors.

Just outside the palace is the Hagia Sophia, the great Byzantine cathedral that took 10,000 men six years to build. For 900 years this church stood for Christianity, then in 1453, Mehmet the Conqueror turned it into a mosque. Today it is a museum. The great edifice seemed to me a tragic symbol of the history of Christ's Church in Turkey. Just as the Christian mosaics of the Hagia Sophia had been plastered over, with minarets added to turn it into a place of worship for Muslims, so had Christianity in Turkey been 'plastered over' and replaced by Islam. But the Church of Jesus Christ had not been destroyed. Obscured for centuries, yes, and oppressed. But one day God would restore it to its rightful place.

7

Walking through the night

Down these mean streets a man must go who is not himself mean, who is neither tarnished nor afraid.
Raymond Chandler, *Atlantic Monthly*

'Oh, no. There's Shelley.' My companion halted, her attention caught by a haggard-looking woman in a white dress and boots. 'She's supposed to be in rehab.' We crossed the street and I watched Christine greet Shelley with a hug. 'I'm waiting for a friend,' the woman told her hastily. After chatting for a moment we walked on. Christine sighed. 'A "friend." That's what she always says.'

It was a raw November night – far too nasty to be touring the back streets of a big city. Montreal has a great deal to offer the visitor, all laced with bilingual charm. But the guidebooks don't usually highlight the stretch along the city's main thoroughfare, St Catherine Street, that intersects 'the village.' This red light district is the haunt of prostitutes, drug dealers, street gangs and other marginals of society who were part of a world that I, like most people I knew, had always carefully avoided. I was about to take a crash course in reality.

The night had begun with prayer and worship in a flat

located inside the village. When the team paired off I found myself the partner of an attractive Australian named Christine Myatt. Christine was one of the most experienced team members of OM Montreal, in charge of the prostitute sector. On this particular night she would introduce me to her 'beat'. After meeting Shelley, Christine took me on a short detour to point out a shop front where a social action group handed out free needles and condoms. Montreal's population included an estimated fifteen thousand heroin-users. 'You'd be surprised if you saw who went in there,' she added. 'Not just street people. Businessmen.' Three or four muscular Hell's Angels lounged in front of a café that we passed. Bikers reputedly owned this part of St Catherine Street. I felt nervous but their attention was fixed on a police cruiser just pulling up. The men melted inside.

We paused to talk to more of Christine's friends. Joanne, a plump blonde in striped shorts, and Gina, a handsome black woman in black tights and mini-skirt, were sheltering in the doorway of a cheap hotel. Christine asked about Joanne's two children, then gave both women an invitation to OM's annual Christmas supper. 'Here they come again,' interrupted Gina suddenly. The women moved out of sight as another police car came up and Christine and I continued along a neon-lit stretch choked with bars, clubs, and sex shops. When we returned ten minutes later Joanne and Gina had been joined by a third woman. 'Miserable night,' I offered awkwardly. What did one say to a prostitute, anyway? The girls nodded agreement and one murmured, 'I don't know what's worse – being cold or being wet.' A passer-by paused to study the trio. Gina smiled at the man, revealing several missing teeth. 'Looking for a good time, honey?'

She took his arm and the pair turned to go inside. Another

of the women held up two fingers, silently inquiring if the customer fancied a second woman. Christine and I walked on.

'We have to be careful not to interfere,' Christine told me matter-of-factly. 'This is their job. And contrary to how the movies show it – girls being forced into prostitution by pimps, against their will – very few of them want to give it up. A lot are hooked on the money. It's an addiction. They can make between $2000 to $3000 a week in this business.' A tall, heavily made-up female passed us clad only in halter top, shorts and pink tights. I shivered, feeling the wind cut through my own warm jacket. 'It's a wonder these girls don't catch pneumonia!' 'They probably do,' Christine replied quietly. She added, 'I think that girl was a transvestite . . . I'm not always sure.'

We had reached the corner of St Catherine and Rue Plessis, the heart of Montreal's village. Of the approximate thirty-eight thousand who lived in the area, 60 to 70 per cent were homosexual. Here and there a male prostitute loitered, hollow-eyed and anorexic-looking in tight jeans. A gay and lesbian poster on the wall advertised forthcoming mass marriage. With a sickening jolt I saw that the artwork included a portrayal of Jesus Christ in a wedding dress. In a tiny nearby park two or three trees fluttered in the streetlight with hundreds of yellow, pink and red ribbons. Each ribbon represented a death, my companion explained. Two and half to three thousand men and women so far had died from AIDS in Quebec. I walked on numbly, past the neon-lit sex shop windows displaying models in chains and leather; the transvestite clubs, gay bars and strip joints. A fine mist surrounded us but I wasn't sure if the wetness on my face was rain or tears. The darkness had closed around my heart. The wailing of police sirens went on and on. And

I thought, 'Dear God, if there is such a place as hell on earth, this must be it.'

It was 1990 when the Montreal team first set out 'to reclaim as many as possible of the inner city's youth for Christ.' A tall order, but the leader of the team knew what he was up against. André Normandin was a child of the Montreal streets himself. After his parents' separation when he was seven he had lived in a series of foster homes and then an orphanage. By the age of eleven André was beating up other kids, and a few years later he slipped into the world of drink and drugs. Burglaries and a bank holdup landed him a jail sentence by his late teens. Afterwards he earned money as a doorman, bartender, drug-pusher and pimp. In 1980, André was in a Florida jail cell for assaulting a police officer, and it was there that he finally hit the wall. 'God, if you are there, get me out of here and I will do whatever you want,' he promised. André was released and less than three years later he was ordained as a Baptist minister. Back in Quebec, the ex-con threw his energies into starting a church and private elementary school. He also led a ministry against cults. But the cry of the streets was too loud to ignore. André began to pray, and a few years later, with only a handful of recruits from OM, he made a start in reaching Montreal's 'untouchables'. 'We made quite a few mistakes to begin with,' admitted Christine, one of the pioneers. 'One skinhead burnt up a Gospel of John with his lighter and said he didn't see Jesus on the streets. So we thought we'd better start by serving people. A few months later we gave a Christmas party and I saw the same guy. I asked why he'd come. He told me, "Because I know you care."'

By the time of my visit OM's ministry had grown to include street kids, homosexuals, and prostitutes. A three month training programme for new recruits incorporated the expertise of police officers, psychologists, and other specialists. In addition, a summer campaign called 'Operation Nineveh' offered exposure to street work for other Christians who were interested.

Campaign director Richard Pare explained: 'We want participants to get a full picture of what happens in the city. Every city in the world is the same. Most people run the other way when they see prostitutes. We need to see them as God sees them. If Jesus was in Montreal, he would go where we go – where there's the most pain.'

Richard knows about pain. He, like André, underwent a radical conversion after being hooked on drugs. During his early days as a Christian he felt like a misfit among the members of his church. The experience hurt. He says he would like to see a church started in the red light district where people would be welcomed just as they are.

Christine's small team concentrated on the city's 5000 to 8000 prostitutes. Most of these girls came from other parts of Canada, runaways or 'throwaways'. Approximately 90 per cent had been sexually abused at home. Runaway girls without job skills are easy prey for pimps. Such girls have a low self-image, and show gratitude for any attention lavished upon them.

Christine explained that most prostitutes fall into one of three general categories. The more exclusive 'call-girls' work through an agency. These women have the benefit of knowing their clients are screened, and are the best protected and best paid. Middle class girls work the streets primarily to support their families; they usually stay away from hard drugs. The majority of lower class hookers are junkies who are working for a fix. 'Where we work they're middle class,' Christine informed me. 'The first contact is hard. There's fear on both sides. You give them your phone number and tell them, "Let me know if you want help in any way." Sometimes we go to the places the girls hang out when they're not working, just to talk and build friendships. We try to go to court with them when they have to appear. One girl asked me, "How can Jesus love me, after what I've done?" We need so much wisdom to know how to answer, not to soften the gospel and not to sound judgmental.' 'They call us the "church girls",' added American co-worker Carrie Abight. 'They ask, "Why do you keep coming back?" What really makes me sad is that a lot of prostitutes have children at home and don't want them to know what they're doing. They want to give them the things they never had. One girl once told me her four-year-old asked where she was going, and why she was putting on all that make-up. "It broke my heart," the girl confessed. "Some day he'll realise what I am. But I don't want my kids ridiculed for being poor."' Carrie shrugged helplessly. 'They're not ready to give up what they're doing.'

Christine's team knows the odds are against them. Only about 5 per cent of prostitutes are 'reachable' – with a genuine desire to get off the streets. And even when they want to, there aren't many places for them to go. 'We need churches to reach out with us. We need them to say: "If a prostitute accepts the Lord, bring her here!"'

'Sometimes I get discouraged. I think, why don't other people come and at least get a glimpse of what's going on? Many times I've prayed, Help me, God, to face another night! A month ago I saw a girl on the street who I thought had gone to Alcoholics Anonymous. She was very drunk. And pregnant. I haven't seen her since. You get scared when you don't see a girl, because anything can happen to them.' But, Carrie and Christine added, there were encouragements too. Being there for the girls, going to court with them, was slowly making an impact. Several were starting to ask questions and read the Bible. A few women had actually left the streets. 'God's teaching me to see past the prostitution to the woman underneath, to the heart,' reflected Christine. 'He's given me a deep love for these women.'

I wondered if the girls on the team were ever afraid as they walked through those mean streets. Had they ever been followed? They replied that they had, once or twice, but they'd lost the men by jumping off suddenly at a metro stop. One day during my visit Carrie showed up with cheeks reddened with cold and announced she had been out walking through the snow flurries, down St Catherine Street. Stopping to admire the Christmas decorations going up she suddenly came upon a woman she knew, sitting on the pavement and weeping. Without thinking Carrie sat down beside her and put her arm around her. There wasn't a lot she could do for the woman but she wanted to show she cared. Gradually she became aware of other passers-by staring at them. 'I wondered what they were thinking,' Carrie shared with us. 'Then suddenly I realised, "I don't care! It doesn't matter what people think!"' She laughed, and I knew as she did that Carrie had achieved an important victory over herself. Perhaps this is what is meant by seeing the world through God's eyes'.

Ron Melanson, leader of the work among street kids, had that same special vision. According to statistics, Montreal's three million-plus residents included 3,000 to 5,000 runaway teenagers. I asked him why. 'It's lack of affection and the need for love that drive a lot of kids to the streets. People don't have to be hungry in Canada – there are shelters and places to get food. The main issue is relational. People are lonely and do whatever it takes to get a "fix" of acceptance. That's what we need to give them.' 'Is it possible to tell which kids you meet are runaways?' I asked. 'You can spot them right away. Most look terrified. Those are the ones you want to get close to because you know what's ahead for them. The experts say that 90 per cent will return home if they're encouraged to during the first three months. After a year that number drops to 20 per cent, and after two years only 5 per cent will ever be reinstated. But going home isn't an option for some kids. They come from really bad situations.'

André Normandin and his team were hoping to open a drop-in centre near St Catherine Street and the gay village during the next year. 'But our outreach on the streets has to keep going,' said Ron. 'Right now I meet most of my contacts in the park or a particular vacant lot. Most are easy to talk to, but you can see them checking you out as you talk. You can't go downtown and wave your Bible around and expect results. There's a time to bring Jesus into the conversation. First you develop a relationship.' Patrick Robitaille was one of the reclaimed ones. I listened to his story when he joined the others for street evangelism one evening. Patrick had been twenty-four and on the streets for about six years when he first met an OM team member. A friendship developed, and after a few years of ups and downs he was ready to turn over his life to Jesus Christ. Patrick was now studying to become a social worker. But such successes took a big investment of time, patience, and tough love. 'Sometimes you feel totally overwhelmed,' reflected Ron. 'You've got to start by putting faces before the statistics. You've got to pray that God will open your heart, and allow you to walk in their shoes. It does something to you. Your love starts to grow.'

I left the city a few days later and took a bus from Canada across the quiet Vermont countryside. Inner city workers were a very special breed of people indeed, I reflected. Yet half of our world would be city-dwellers by the year 2000. How many would get lost in the darkness of our cities' back streets? And how many of us would have the courage to walk through the night, for Jesus' sake, to find them?

8

Land of promise

*The word Palestine always brought to my mind a vague
suggestion of a country as large as the United States.
I do not know why, but such was the case. I suppose
it was because I could not conceive of a small country
having so large a history.*

Mark Twain, *The Innocents Abroad*

Our bus paused at the entrance to Ben Gurion International
Airport. A security guard boarded, glanced around, then
suddenly froze, erupting in rapid Hebrew. The other passengers grabbed their belongings and left. I decided I'd
better follow. More soldiers appeared from all directions,
waving us back behind a barrier. Sirens screamed, a bomb
unit arrived and airport traffic backed up for miles.

A German tourist who had, like me, stowed her luggage
in the bus's undercarriage stood beside me wringing her
hands. 'My souvenirs,' she moaned. 'My souvenirs!' I could
understand her chagrin. My precious film – the only visual
record I had of four weeks of travel – appeared in imminent
jeopardy of being blown up. The other passengers wore a
look of patient resignation that told me they had been
through this routine before. A few days ago, they said,

a bus outside Tel Aviv had been blown up. This time we were lucky. The soldiers eventually gave the all-clear and allowed us to resume our journey. Such was part of everyday life in Israel.

The episode seemed like an appropriate finale to my first visit to this country. As a journalist I had found it exhilarating to be in the eye of the hurricane. Jewish–Arab emotion was running high over the handing back of the Gaza Strip and Jericho. The debate over the Golan Heights continued to rage, and the stepped-up violence of Hamas terrorists after the recent Hebron massacre was putting everyone on edge. But as a Christian, as well as the daughter of a Jew, Israel hit me between the eyes with an impact I hadn't expected.

I'd arrived at Ben Gurion a month before, delighted to exchange the London fog for palm trees and sunshine. Workers in the country had assured me that spring was the best possible season to taste this land of milk and honey. During March and April, they said, the hillsides were ablaze with wildflowers that would perish during the intense heat of summer. And the Arab souks overflow with succulent fruits and vegetables. They were right. As we left the airport my excited cries amused my friends. There were roadsigns pointing toward Jaffa, others directed us to Dan, Ashdod, and Beersheba. These were names I had known since childhood. I felt like a blind person who was suddenly able to see the face of a familiar friend. Like most first-time visitors I was startled to see so many soldiers everywhere, M-16 rifles casually slung over their shoulders. All eighteen-year-olds were expected to serve in the army or IDF – Israel Defence Forces. Wherever I travelled I noticed uniformed young people hitching rides to or from their posts of duty.

My first stop was the industrial port of Haifa. Although Haifa is too modern to earn a mention in the Bible, most of the city climbs the lower slopes of ancient Mount Carmel – which is not a single peak at all but an entire range. Haifa appears a very secular city, with very few Jewish men sporting the round skullcap, *kippa*, that is the trademark of the religious. Arabs and Jews work together quite amicably. In fact, the most impressive building in Haifa is neither a temple nor a mosque but the gold-domed world headquarters of the Baha'i. I was more impressed at the compound I was visiting. Although it resembled hundreds of others built into the steeply terraced hillside, this particular house had once offered hospitality to Hannah Hurnard, author of the well-known *Hind's Feet on High Places*. The peaceful garden of geraniums, calla lilies and almond trees must have been a source of great pleasure. Unfortunately, the compound was now scarred by a concrete bomb shelter.

During my stay I listened to friends describe what it had been like during the tension-filled days of the Gulf War. Inside the shelter I could almost hear the wailing sirens that had shocked them from sleep, night after night. I could almost see them groping for their gas masks and torches and stumbling through the blackness to safety. They and another family had survived eighteen Scud missile attacks from Iraq inside this grim little box. At the end of each attack the two men, Colin and David, had taken turns to emerge first from the shelter, just in case there had been a release of poison gas. Although thirty-nine of the missiles fell on unpopulated areas or were intercepted by US Patriot missiles, several bombs landed on populated areas where they inflicted heavy damage. Altogether, Israel endured without retaliation thirteen deaths and 200 injuries.

But this weekend of 1994 all thoughts were focused on

Passover, the 5,754th commemoration of the Jewish flight from Egypt. What an honour it was for me to be here, sharing the Seder feast with about forty others who had come to recognise Jesus Christ as their Passover Lamb! And as we concluded our simple and joyful meal together, we lifted our voices in a heartfelt prayer: 'May we celebrate the Seder next year in the new Jerusalem!'

That first *Shabat*, or Sabbath, I attended a thriving Messianic fellowship built high on top of Mount Carmel. The service, conducted in both English and Hebrew, had an exuberance that embraced us all. Afterwards, my hosts introduced me to worshippers who had emigrated from Australia, America, Japan, and South Africa. I marvelled again at this young country that had opened its arms to the world. Following the service we drove to the Druze village of Daliyat to collect a picnic of felafel – deep-fried chick-peas and spices rolled in delicious flat bread – before heading for the famous peak where Elijah defied the priests of Baal. A monastery now guards the site and visitors are obliged to pay an entrance fee, but the view is worth it. Standing on this windy precipice I could see the whole Jezreel Valley, and the hills of Nazareth beyond. At this time of year all was lushly carpeted in green. A large and prosperous kibbutz lay in the heart of the valley, and from below us drifted the sound of lowing cows. It was hard to picture a scene more at odds with the terrible fate predicted for it in the Scriptures, where it is called the Valley of Armageddon.

Passover week is a holiday for many Jews, and one of my purposes in coming to Israel at this time was to join a special evangelistic outreach around the Sea of Galilee. We were on our way to the kibbutz where we would be staying when our team van suddenly pulled off the road. I saw that other vehicles had also stopped, presumably for the view.

No one enlightened me until we all got out and walked to an elevated point that sloped gently to the lake. This, they smiled, was the Mount of the Beatitudes. The team found a quiet place where the birds sang and the wind stirred the trees, and together we read Jesus's words to his disciples: 'Blessed are you when people insult you, persecute you and falsely say all kinds of evil against you because of me . . . for in the same way they persecuted the prophets who were before you' (Matt 5: 11–12). The words were to sustain us in the days ahead. Tiberias, the main town on the lake, was at one time the seat of the Sanhedrin and remains to this day a bastion of ultra-Orthodox Judaism. All of us on the team were aware that the message we carried would not be any more popular than it was during Jesus's day.

It seemed right when our eleven-member team was rounded up to twelve in Tiberias. Tanya, a sixteen-year-old Russian Jewish believer, was the only local church member who chose to join our outreach. Their response was perhaps understandable since they had once been deliberately burned out of their first place of worship. To our great relief, however, our open-air programmes in the town went off without much opposition. Some of the leaflets we distributed, which simply reproduced Isaiah 53 in Hebrew, were torn up without more than a glance. But occasionally an individual would stop to read it, and consider the question, 'Who exactly does this passage in the *Tenach* refer to?' I liked to walk up to people after the team finished distributing leaflets in an area. 'Hello, I'm an American journalist,' I would brazenly introduce myself. 'I'm just visiting Tiberias. Do you mind if I ask you a few questions?' Invariably, if the person understood me, they were happy to practise their English and never bothered to ask for my credentials. Many of the younger people I talked to were *sabras* – Israeli born – with their parents coming from countries like Morocoo, Iran, and Iraq. I asked them what the leaflet they'd received was about and what they thought of it. Sometimes I went on to share about my own search for truth, and how it had ended at the feet of *Yeshua*, Jesus.

Israelis occasionally exhibit a boldness or aggressiveness of manner that takes visitors aback. This *chutzpah* is probably a reflection of the nation's long struggle to achieve an identity. In Israel there is no polite standing in bus queues, or shy hanging back from conversation with strangers. In this country you must be prepared to give as well as take or you won't be respected – nor will you discover the warmth that lies just below the intimidating surface. During my visit I grew to enjoy and even admire the Israeli chutzpah. I suspect this came from harbouring a trace of it myself! A young Swiss colleague told me that on a bus trip from Tel Aviv he once found himself the subject of an inquisition by the Jewish lady beside him. After putting him through a complete inventory of his work, home, family, and religion, the woman apparently decided Felix would do – she proposed that he marry her daughter!

After a few days in Tiberias the team moved out along the shores of Lake Galilee. Walking two by two and stopping to chat with people and distribute booklets in the picnic and swimming areas, we were more than ever grateful to have Tanya with us – a number of the families we encountered were Russian, and without exception they were delighted to receive books and Bibles in their own language. Russian immigration was in fact having a massive impact on the country. Predictions were that by the year 2000, one fifth of Israel's population would be Russian.

Besides Russians, our international group met Arab and Druze holiday-makers and a number of secular Jews who were happy to converse. Two team-mates from South Africa and Denmark spent an hour with two soldiers who were patrolling the beach. The men accepted a book of testimonies by Messianic believers, and addresses were exchanged. The only really nasty encounter occurred on the third day. Daniel, from England, was offering literature to picnickers when he was suddenly attacked by three ultra-Orthodox Jews. The men backed Daniel against a van with their fingers at his throat. Wanda, his partner, stood watching helplessly until the three finally let him go with a few threats, only 'because he was with a woman'. The incident shook me more than it did Daniel. Although he got off unharmed, I knew of team members who had been badly beaten and even stoned in the past. It gave me a glimpse of what it cost to live as a disciple of Christ in this land.

Shopping in Jewish supermarkets during Passover was unlike shopping anywhere else. Any food product with even a trace of yeast was forbidden throughout the week, which meant whole aisles were covered over. I was surprised to learn just how many items were involved. Bread, of course, could only be found in Arab areas. After close to a week of matzo crackers we decided to splash out on pizza in Tiberias. Wrong move. Unleavened pizza might bring joy to the hearts of the faithful, but I can't imagine it does the same for their stomachs!

Before leaving Lake Galilee we drove our van up to the Golan Heights. Wildflowers did their best to hide the scars of war on the windswept plateau, but the shelled ruins of homes were everywhere. So were the barbed-wire fences and posted mine warnings. Near the Syrian border we stopped to look over at an entire deserted city in the 'no-man's land' near a UN encampment. Standing there it was easy to comprehend the hurt and bitterness of the Syrians, who had once looked upon this place as home. But gazing down upon the lushly cultivated Jordan Valley I could also understand Israel's reluctance to give the territory back. Whoever commanded the heights would also control the valley. Syria's repossession would create an obvious security risk. Like most people, when I thought of Israel I had tended to think only of the Jewish population. My perspective was widening. Eighteen per cent or almost one fifth of Israel's residents, I now realised, were Druze or Bedouin, Muslim or Christian Arabs.

Jesus's own home town, once only a huddle of houses in the Galilean hills, is in fact predominantly Arab. I travelled there hoping to experience at least some of the ambience of biblical days, but like every other tourist I was disappointed. Modern Nazareth is concrete and commercial, with tall apartment buildings built into the hills, housing over fifty thousand residents. The main tourist attraction is the Basilica of the Annunication. The money lavished on this church, said to be built on the spot where Gabriel told Mary she was to conceive a son, was utterly amazing. Yet to me the most moving place to visit in Nazareth is a very old stone synagogue near the souk. It was to this small temple that the young Jesus came to worship with his father. And it was here that the boy became a man, the teacher who announced one Sabbath to his fellow Jews: 'Today this scripture is fulfilled in your hearing' (Luke 4:21).

Comparatively few Christian workers in Israel are concerned with reaching out to Arabs. Those who do invest a great part of their time in learning fluent Arabic so that they can build friendships, the heart of Arab ministry. I listened as one worker expressed his frustration over the fact that no one was sharing the gospel to Israel's 80,000 Druze. The Druze people were an offshoot of the Muslim community, holding their own secret beliefs. At this time no Christian literature existed in the Druze language. It would be another year or two before a simple gospel tract would finally be produced. In fact many of Israel's 'Christian' Arabs are actually non-Muslims with no strong faith of any kind. Such men and women are ripe for a confrontation with the living Christ. As it is, girls from nominal Christian families are often given in marriage to Muslim men.

Of course, no trip to Israel can be complete without at least a glimpse of the capital city. I had cherished little hope of visiting Jerusalem during Easter, knowing that every available bed would be booked far in advance, even if I could afford one! But somehow the impossible happened. Accommodation was found at the last moment with the gracious friend of a friend who lived outside the city. In addition to that, I was lucky enough to have the companionship of an OMer who knew her way around. Rain was bucketing down when René and I arrived at Jerusalem's central bus station on Good Friday afternoon. We took shelter in a coffee shop, watching soldiers and Orthodox Jews hurrying in all directions. I was captivated by the variety of the Hasidim's black coats, beards and round fur hats – the latter looking slightly ridiculous with their waterproof wrappings. Husbands and wives were invariably surrounded by hordes of children, all neatly dressed. Women who were not wearing hats or scarves all seemed to sport the same chin-length hairstyle. René explained to me that these were wigs, the Orthodox wife's only alternative to covering her natural hair in public! Since the rain showed no signs of slacking off we decided a bus tour was the only practical option for taking an overall look at the city. Unfortunately the windows of our coach steamed up so we didn't see much of anything, and in the sudden rush to leave the tour at the last stop, I left a borrowed sleeping bag under a seat! All attempts to retrieve it failed, and I ended up having to buy another one.

In spite of the unpromising start, our spirits rose with the sun the next day. René and I found a ride into the city and walked though the Jewish quarter, quiet and shuttered for the Sabbath. The Arab bazaar was quite the opposite; we joined the crowds surging through the narrow passageways, pausing frequently to admire jewellery, pottery and stalls crammed with myriads of other interesting items. Later René admitted that she had received instructions to keep an eye on me in the souk. I looked Jewish, she said, and tensions were running high.

We had hoped to attend the sunrise service at the garden tomb on Easter Sunday, but transport from our accommodation proved impossible. I was very glad that we had chosen to visit the garden the day before. On Saturday the grounds were surprisingly uncrowded, the shady paths restful and unspoiled. The tomb itself would be closed to the public on Sunday because of the sheer volume of visitors. When I came upon the place, cut into the rocky face of a hill and looking quite unremarkable, a group of tourists had arrived before me. I waited until they left, and then stepped into the small, cool chamber alone.

> Amazing love, O what sacrifice,
> The Son of God given for me.
> My debt He pays and my death He dies,
> That I might live, that I might live.

The words of Graham Kendrick seemed to swell and fill the silence – was it a celestial choir of thousands or only the singing of my own heart? I stood before the crude stone shelf where, it was believed, the body of my Lord had been laid after his crucifixion. Tears came to my eyes as I remembered all he had gone through for me. The tears fell as I thought of the millions who still refused to accept that his act of love was for them too. I turned to leave, and my eyes fell on an inscription on the door: 'He is not here, for he is risen!' My grief was suddenly forgotten in a rush of gladness. The empty tomb was not a place of mourning: its very emptiness sang of victory! Those who came to this place were meant to celebrate. Jesus Christ had conquered death. His mission was accomplished.

Later that afternoon, René and I came to a security checkpoint where Israeli soldiers searched us closely. We were then allowed into one of the holiest places on earth for all Jews: the courtyard before the Wailing Wall of the old temple. I had seen this wall countless times in photographs and on TV. Now I actually stood in the women's section with my hands against the worn stone, listening to the prayers of young and old all around me. More blood had been shed at the gates of Jerusalem than any other city on earth – and the fighting was not yet over. Quietly I added my petition to the others, asking God to bring healing through the One who is our peace.

But the extraordinary weekend was not yet over. On Easter Sunday René took me outside the encircling walls of the old city, and we climbed part of the way up the Mount of Olives. The Garden of Gethsemane's most ancient olive trees were now fenced off for protection, but the garden was still a fragrant, flower-filled oasis. Past the souvenir-sellers outside and further up the hill we sat under another olive tree to eat our lunch. What a view! Directly facing us, across the Kidron Valley, was Jerusalem's 'Golden Gate' – the famous sealed entrance which, according to the Bible, would open one day to receive the King of Kings.

In the words of W.M. Thomson the City of David, hub of faith for Jew, Muslim and Christian alike, was 'By far the most interesting half-acre on the face of the earth.' I deeply regretted that we were unable to explore it all. And yet, I don't believe I could have absorbed any more that I did in the space of this one weekend. The city had 3,000 years of history after all. But I had spent this one Easter of my life in Jerusalem, and with that I could be content.

While I was in Israel I was able to attend exuberant Arab evangelistic fellowships as well as Messianic Jewish churches. The highlight of them all, however, had to be the area of Galilee's Women's gathering, which periodically brings Arab and Jewish women together as one in Christ. I was thrilled to be among them; and I am convinced their prayers for Israel's peace have been responsible for far more change than any official handshakes between heads of state.

Walking down David Ben Gurion Street in Haifa just before Independence Day I saw flags flying from street lights, buildings and passing vehicles alike. I smiled at this enthusiastic display of nationalism, and felt I was beginning to understand it. I had been in so many places where the Jewish minority had to choose between keeping their faith a secret or else suffering contempt or abuse. Israel was the only country in the world where Jews could shout their identity from the housetops without fear. They had fought and waited for that privilege for a very long time, and they would never give it up.

It was time to gather up all my notes and souvenirs – everything but my film – and pack them into a large mailing bag. From Israel I was planning to travel to Egypt and then, if I had sufficient time, to Jordan; so no trace of anything Israeli could be left in my bags. When a friend who was flying to Ireland offered to post everything to my office in London, I accepted gratefully. This arrangement would surely be safer than posting the package all the way from Israel. But I was wrong. Royal Mail officials admitted weeks later that my package had somehow vanished between Dublin and London. All efforts to trace it failed. I was distraught. All the interviews, the notes I'd worked so hard to gather during my time in Israel could never be recovered.

From a journalist's point of view, the trip was perhaps a disaster. But on a deeper, more personal level I could hardly regret this assignment. Israel had become a nation the same year I was born. I had always felt a link, and now I knew I could never again regard it dispassionately. This land and the welfare of its people had become important to me. Israel was now a part of me.

9

Flight to Egypt

*Cairo . . . the metropolis of the universe, the garden of
the world, the anthill of the human species . . .*

Ibn Kaldun

Being checked through Israel's security for my flight to
Egypt was the nightmare my fellow workers had warned
me of. Single women travelling alone in the Middle East
are automatically targets of suspicion. I was subjected to an
interrogation that would have made Mother Theresa sweat.
The fact was, although I was no threat to national security
I wasn't eager to reveal names and addresses of people
I'd stayed with. Information on Christian workers could
endanger their visa status. But the inspectors weren't happy
with my vague answers. They were particularly critical when
I could show them nothing to back my claim that I was a
writer. I'd left my business cards home since they carried
a mission logo, and all my notebooks had been sent back
to Britain.

My two pieces of luggage and shoulder-bag were con-
sequently torn apart and their contents examined and
x-rayed, item by item. One inspector was unfamiliar with the
newest style of carry-on cases with wheels and a retractable

tow-handle built into the frame. He demanded to know why I was using this kind of luggage instead of a backpack. I squeaked indignantly that my brother had given it to me as a present. He whisked it into a back room to have it x-rayed. Several hours later I was finally escorted to the check-in counter and out of the security area. I'd passed! I collapsed in a waiting area, clutching the ballpoint pen I'd been presented with by the airport authority as a token of thanks for my patience. The pen stopped working after a few weeks, but I couldn't bring myself to throw it away.

The flight to Cairo passed uneventfully. Within two hours the plane was descending, the sun and sand coming up to meet me, and I was landing in an alien world. I had done my homework before visiting the ancient land of the Pharoahs. I knew ninety-five per cent of it is desert, and whatever is green – along with most of the population – clings for life to the River Nile. But the reality of Egypt dazzled my eyes, gritted my skin and turned my hair to straw. A terrible thirst assailed me and for the whole of my stay I guzzled water like a camel that could never get enough.

Staying with Christian workers in Egyptian-style accommodation offers insights on everyday life that ordinary tourists, ensconced in the Sheraton Hotel, are denied. One learns about filtering water before drinking it, heating water to wash clothes, and coping with the layers of dust that appeared daily on all surfaces no matter how regularly they were cleaned. The first evening I sat on a flat rooftop overlooking the city, talking for a long time with the women on the team. When I finally bid my hostess good night she gave me an anxious smile. 'I hope you sleep well,' she told me. Lying in the sweltering heat without the benefit of a fan or air-conditioning, and on a mattress which was about as comfy as a tablet of stone, I began to understand that smile.

The shutters were open, but instead of a longed-for breeze I was treated to an unrelenting cacophony of barking dogs, blaring traffic, and shouting passers-by. Just before dawn as I was sinking into a troubled sleep, a terrific din erupted all over the city. The noise seemed to gather momentum until it reached a crescendo: the 4.15 a.m. call to prayer. Unfortunately the mullahs of the surrounding mosques hadn't synchronised their watches. Just as the recording of the chant ceased from one loudspeaker, another took it up. And Cairo is, without doubt, 'the city of a thousand minarets'!

Expatriate friends later assured me that during the month of Ramadan, when Muslims observe a fast between sunrise and sunset, it was even worse – a caller had come through their streets to awaken everyone for breakfast at about 2 a.m.! After several weeks of disturbed sleep they'd had enough. They enquired how much the man was being paid to do his job, then offered him twice the amount to stop. He only laughed. My first morning's call to prayer was soon followed by the shouts of men and boys selling produce in the streets. By 6 a.m. I gave up the battle, my bones bruised from a night of uncomfortable shifting, and my ears sore from efforts to block out the noise.

If the Nile is the circulatory system through which Egypt's life has flowed for 7000 years, Cairo is its heart. Designed for only 4,000,000 people, the city pulses with four times that number, and expands by another million each year. Patience is definitely the quality to develop in Cairo. Getting to any destination will take more time than you expect. Taxi and bus horns are employed non-stop as their owners attempt to avoid collisions and attract customers. Pavements, where they exist, are usually usurped by cars that are double-or even triple-parked with breaks disengaged so they can, if necessary, be rolled out of the way.

One plus is Cairo's metro system: fast, modern and simple to use, with the names of stops written in English as well as Arabic. Tickets to any destination cost no more than twenty pence. In deference to Muslim propriety, the first carriage is always reserved for women. Once I packed into this overcrowded carriage the same time as an unfortunate male, who immediately found himself the target of outraged cries. He escaped the next time the doors opened. I studied the fifty or sixty other women crammed into the airless compartment. Many were swathed in traditional black from head to toe, with even their hands covered with thick black gloves. I was perspiring profusely dressed only in a light cotton dress! Schoolgirls and some of the younger women wore a less severe, light-coloured caftan, or even a modest Western-style skirt and blouse with a white scarf covering their hair. Perhaps it's the heavy prohibitions on women's dress that make the men appear, in contrast, so fashionable. The majority of professional workers are very sharp dressers indeed. I couldn't repress a chuckle each time I came upon clusters of such men window-shopping, stopping to gaze admiringly at some shoe or clothing display!

After travelling in other Muslim countries I was pleasantly surprised at how secure I felt in getting about Cairo on my own. My light complexion and dark hair allowed me to pass for an upper class Egyptian, so I usually escaped harrassment. Women who are more obviously outsiders, with blonde hair or Asian features, are not always so fortunate. Foreigners are generally regarded as easy targets. When I asked a Western worker what bothered her the most about living in Egypt, she instantly responded, 'The men! It takes a lot of grace not to hit them sometimes.' She went on to explain that it was impossible to treat male acquaintances with the same casual friendliness she was accustomed to using with men at home. 'You have to ignore them – act almost rude to them – or they may show up the next day with gifts and ask to marry you. Even if they already have a wife and children!' I was inclined to believe her observation, since I myself had received a proposal within my first few hours of landing in Egypt!

With childbearing the *raison d'être* for women in this society, most girls marry very young. Colleagues told me ruefully that single women, and even women who are married but have no children, are accorded little respect. Only when a wife bears her first child (preferably male) does she earn the title 'Om', which means 'mother of', followed by the child's name. In her book about Egyptian women, *Khul-Khaal*, Nayra Atiya explains: 'Om shows that a woman has fulfilled her calling, that of becoming a mother. Sometimes a childless woman will be called "mother of the absent one" in order not to use her first name, which would show disrespect or belittle her.'

I was distressed to learn how widely the practice of female circumcision is still practised among Egypt's poorer classes. Little girls as young as five are subjected to this cruel act of mutilation, in the belief that it will keep them chaste for their husbands. Although the tradition is not endorsed by the Koran, centuries of folklore and superstition are difficult to overturn. In fact, in spite of protests by human rights groups, a prominent fundamentalist mullah recently went on record to endorse female circumcision.

Another evidence of folk Islam's power over everyday life is the universal fear of the 'evil eye'. No one, even among the upper classes, would consider expressing admiration for a newborn baby – or, indeed, any prized possession – unless he or she meant to bring harm upon it. Amulets to ward off the power of the jealous and ill-wishing, such as blue beads or replicas of an eye, are in evidence in many parts of the Middle East.

It's easy to forget that Christianity actually preceded Islam in Egypt by six centuries. Years after Mary and Joseph took refuge there with Jesus, the Apostle Mark returned with the gospel message. But when Islam came to northern Africa, it conquered the area. Egypt is officially a secular state but the law punishes anyone who 'offends' Islam with five years in prison. Those who attempt to convert a Muslim can be sentenced to three years in jail. On the other hand, it's common practice for fundamentalist Muslims to discriminate against Christians. An estimated twelve thousand Copts convert each year in order to obtain jobs or promotions. Christians are not allowed to build or even repair their meeting-places without a government permit – and no such permits have been issued for over twelve years. During that same period, more than eighty thousand new mosques have appeared on the skyline. All Christian churches are known to have at least two or three informers among their members. Fellowships may be – and sometimes are – closed overnight, with no explanation. Telephones are frequently tapped, and individuals watched or followed. Under such circumstances, believers are understandably wary of sharing the gospel with their Muslim neighbours. But that picture is slowly changing. Within a number of churches small cells of people are meeting to receive practical evangelism training. And they are beginning to reach out.

Extremes of wealth and destitution co-exist within Cairo. The city that boasts over two hundred thousand millionaires also contains vast slums with 60,000 men, women and children per square mile. Ten years ago some of the members of a Christian mission committed themselves to living at the level of these poorest of the poor, in order to share Jesus Christ. I visited one family who had made their home in the slums for five years.

Frank and Elsa and their two little girls had worked hard at becoming part of their community. They spoke fluent Arabic, dressed like their neighbours, shopped where they did and ate the same foods. A fifty-year-old washing-machine was the only concession to luxury in their tiny flat.

Elsa told me that during the summer months the heat rose to over 43°C. 'Cleaning is much harder here with all the dust,' she conceded ruefully. 'I've had to give up my high standards!' Because running water was only available at 8 or 9 p.m. and in summer not until 12 or 1 a.m., most of her washing and cleaning had to be done at night. I asked Frank and Elsa why they felt it was important to identify so closely with their neighbours. 'There's a deep rift between Muslim and Christian communities,' Frank explained, 'and it's not all to do with Jesus. It has to do with the clothes you wear, the food you eat, and a lot of other things. We have decided to belong to the Muslim community, and Jesus Christ and his cross will be the only stumbling-block between us.'

'To be invited into an Egyptian's life you have to prove your friendship,' added another woman on the team. 'You must become vulnerable – cry with them, and laugh with them. You can't just defend yourself all the time as a Christian to Muslims. They have many misconceptions. You must find things they believe that you also believe, and be patient. Show what God's love is. I haven't seen anyone come to faith yet, but that's God's job. We just have to trust.'

I walked through the City of the Dead, the cemetery taken

over by Cairo's destitute. This was where the team had first begun, each member learning what it was to live with only the bare necessities until – as the founder put it – they no longer refer to the poor as 'them' but 'us'. I came away from these men and women feeling humbled. How many of us would have the courage to incarnate the gospel, wrap it up in ourselves and deliver it, at such a price?

On the other hand, Cairo has no shortage of Islamic fundamentalists who will do anything to promote their faith. One evening I had dinner with an attractive Muslim woman named Manal. Manal had somehow achieved the impossible by reaching the age of twenty-seven without being married. She was a laboratory research assistant and, although she had agreed to accept the marriage proposal of a colleague during the coming year, they would both continue pursuing doctoral studies.

For most of the evening I listened, fascinated, to this highly intelligent woman. Her argument was that Judaism lay at the root of all that was wrong with the world. Since she knew that I had just come from Israel, I ventured to ask her about the recent Hamas bombings. Her expression went blank. 'Hamas? Who are they?' I couldn't believe Manal did not know of the group's existence. Perhaps she knew them by a different name. 'They're Palestinian extremists. Terrorists. I was in Nazareth when they bombed a Jewish bus just a few miles to the south.' 'They couldn't be Muslims,' she declared. 'Muslims don't murder, unless they have to repay other murders. That's only justice.' 'What about all the tourist buses that have been attacked here in Egypt?' I asked. That, according to Manal, was Israel's fault too. The Jews were coming from Israel and trying to cause problems. Things would never be right until a strong Muslim government took power. I decided I'd had enough, and tried a different tack. 'Manal, my father is Jewish.' She paled. 'You said you were a Christian!' 'I am a follower of *Issa* – Jesus – that's true. I don't think we should automatically adopt the religion of our fathers without thinking things through for ourselves. Do you? Manal, have you ever talked to a Jew, face to face?' She conceded that she hadn't. 'You know, there are a lot of people in the West where I'm from, who have never met a Muslim. They have a lot of strange ideas about what Muslims are like. Don't you think some of the problems in the world might come from not really knowing each other?' Manal was clearly embarrassed. She was certain I would be furious about what she'd said, so I tried hard to show her I wasn't. I think we parted as friends, but for us both, the evening was a revelation.

The differences in the Eastern calendar gave me the chance to celebrate a second Easter in Cairo. When we heard that Handel's *Messiah* would be performed in the international church, my friend Vera and I went to hear it.

There is nothing like being surrounded by millions of people who know or care nothing for Jesus Christ to infuse the message of that famous oratorio with new meaning. The experience was like gulping a glass of cold, refreshing water on a desert island. I didn't know how thirsty I had been until that moment. It was all I could do not to jump to my feet and burst out singing with the choir. I wanted to shout the words from the rooftop, and affirm their truth to all those in Egypt who sat in darkness:

> *And He shall reign, forever and ever.*
> *King of Kings, and Lord of Lords!*

Amen. So he shall. And every knee shall bow and every tongue confess who he is.

Of course, it is unthinkable for anyone to leave a place like Cairo without spending at least one day on the tourist trail. Two long-term workers, Vera and Letitia, volunteered to escort me and we all voted to wear trousers for the occasion. Not the most culturally sensitive choice, but trousers *were* occasionally seen in the streets and they would certainly make sense if we should end up riding camels. The morning was devoted to *Khan al Khalili*. The most famous of all Cairo's bazaars was a shopper's paradise, overflowing with the garish and the magnificent, everything from papyrus to perfume. We took a break for coffee in a café that was heavy with atmosphere. Watching the customers around us lazily smoking hookahs I could almost believe myself in another time and place. If a reclining customer had snapped their fingers and belly dancers appeared, I wouldn't have been at all surprised.

Back in the market we ran into a gaggle of tourists whose short shorts made our trio look positively nunlike. I was indignant. Visitors who refused to show any respect for local conventions only reinforced the Egyptians' belief that all Western women were immoral. We were loath to leave the bazaar, and by the time we tore ourselves away and reached Giza, it was too late to go inside the pyramids. I wasn't really too disappointed. Just to stand before them and look up at their awesome splendour was enough. The wonder of the pyramids cannot possibly be conveyed by photographs. 'Forty centuries of history looking down on us,' as Napoleon remarked to his army. I only wish that we could have been left to ourselves to enjoy the sight, but children and adults, thick as flies and just as persistent, buzzed around us competing for attention.

Most Egyptians are disarmingly eager to try out their varying amounts of English. Everywhere you go you are likely to be assaulted by phrases like 'Welcome to Egypt!' 'What is your name?' or 'What time is it?' But this was not the place for banal chit-chat. I made for the nearest 'rent-a-camel' and clambered aboard. The Bedouin who owned the beast would not be content until I had also donned a filthy robe and head-dress and brandished a crop like the Sheikh of Araby. The camel had the cheek to laugh at my imitation – a raucous noise that almost made me lose my lunch – and then it lurched clumsily to its feet. I hung on for dear life, certain each moment was the last, until suddenly I found myself enjoying the experience. I did feel like a sheikh! – the burning sun, the blowing sand exhilarated me . . . I was ready to ride off into the sunset when my noble steed decided I'd had my money's worth and sank to its knees. Only by the greatest good fortune did I avoid sailing over his head.

The guide-books declare that sunset is one of the best times of day to view the sphinx and pyramids. We lingered long enough to prove them right. The spectacle of those massive stone edifices in dramatic silhouette against the fiery sky sent shivers through me. The sense of timelessness must be experienced to be understood. To cap a fairy-tale day the three of us hired a *felucca* for an evening sail on the Nile. As the sails filled with a refreshing breeze, I felt like pinching myself. Here we were gliding through the heart of 7000-year-old Cairo. With the stars overhead and the lights of the city twinkling all around us it was easy to believe this was the real setting for the adventures of the Arabian Nights. Afterwards we stopped to assuage our hunger at an Egyptian restaurant, then headed home to wash away the day's accumulation of sand.

Registering at the passport office in El Tahrir Square some days later gave me the opportunity to duck into the nearby

Egyptian Antiquities Museum for a few hours. For me and most other visitors the highlight of this treasure-house is the Tutankhamun exhibition. I happened to be in London several years before when the British Museum exhibited the discovery, but the queues had been far too long. What a pleasure to be able to gaze my fill at the gold and the jewels here in Egypt, with no need to queue and at a fraction of the entrance fee!

By this time it was obvious I would have to scratch Jordan from my itinerary. There simply wasn't time to go there and cover our work adequately. I finished my interviews in Cairo and made a quick trip to see workers in Alexandria. Then I booked a seat on a coach back to Tel Aviv airport. Cairo was then in the throes of a heat wave that was making even the residents stagger, so I got very little sleep on my last night there. I rose in good time for the taxi that was ordered for 4.30 a.m. After creeping down the apartment stairs in the pitch dark, however – the electricity being off – my friend Vera and I waited in vain until 4.50 a.m. Vera was clad only in a nightdress and robe (which, however, is considered perfectly respectable at that hour; I had seen men outdoors in their pyjamas!). She instructed me to stay with the luggage and set off for the main road to hail another taxi. When a gang of vicious dogs spotted her, barking and circling ominously, my heart was in my throat. But Vera ran the gauntlet successfully. She reappeared five minutes later with a taxi whose driver was delighted to find such a good fare.

I made it on time to the coach departure point and noticed several armed guards standing around, a grim reminder of the recent attacks by Muslim extremists. Our bus would be travelling in convoy with other buses as far as the Israeli border. Would we circle up like a wagon train, I wondered, if we were attacked? A companion to the driver had a gun stuck into his belt and I realised I had only a dozen fellow passengers for the long ride ahead. Maybe the bus hadn't been such a good idea. But a hundred miles later we pulled up at the Suez Canal and waited for a ferry to take us across. I was thrilled. I had never yet travelled through the famous canal but at least I was going across it. When we reached the other side, we were met by the Sinai.

The desert was everything I had pictured it would be, an endless wilderness of sand broken only by an occasional oasis, and camels grazing on whatever scrub they could find. Here and there Bedouin women and children herded sheep and goats near isolated enclosures constructed of palm branches. Their homes were tents or the simplest of houses. After a couple of hundred miles of this amazing landscape I almost regretted reaching the Egyptian–Israeli border. Security inspections took several hot and sweaty hours, then all passengers were transferred to an Israeli bus for the few hours remaining to Tel Aviv.

The exodus through the desert had provided a satisfying finale to my assignment. By the time my plane left Israel at 3 a.m. I was shattered. The grilling by the airport authorities was just as intensive – if not more so – as my previous one. I didn't even get another pen for my pains! But the Middle East had worked its magic on me. *In sha'allah* – God willing – I would someday return.

10

The mustard seed conspiracy

While millions sat glued to their TVs watching the World Cup during the summer of 1994, 1400 men and women from fifty-six nations opted for action of their own. OM's annual Love Europe programme promises young Christians travel, training, teamwork, and a tantalising taste of mission. But along with fun in the sun the summer delivers some powerful truths about the way God can use ordinary people.

'We are part of the mustard seed conspiracy,' Love Europe Director Stuart McAllister told volunteers at the initial orientation weeks in Sweden and Germany. 'God is sending us out all over Europe as mustard seeds, planting new life. Can you make a difference? Absolutely, if you go out in faith, not fear!' This was the fourth time I had covered Love Europe, but the final night of the training congress gripped me once again with the same electric excitement.

'Let me be a shining light to the nations, a shining light to the people of the world!' The singing that burst from the huge old barn in Torp, Sweden, should have splintered the timbers. As a procession of flag-bearers wound their way up to the stage the MC announced each target country. Team members stood for a prayer of commitment. Within a few hours they would be streaming away from the congress centre to all points of the compass. Teams of one to six weeks' duration, dedicated to spreading mustard seeds of faith as far as Murmansk, Russia, above the Arctic Circle, and Kazakhstan in Central Asia.

My assignment this year was to report on some of the action in Scandinavia and the Baltics. Photographer Tim Wright and his wife Linda, who had travelled with me in Turkey, were once again to be my companions. We drove first to Norway, then turned back to visit several teams in Sweden and Finland. Two of these countries were new to me and I was delighted by their similarity to my own beloved New England. Deep lakes and thickly forested mountains – even glimpses of moose and deer – made me feel right at home. So did the people. Judging by the hospitality we encountered, Love Europe participants linked with Scandinavian churches were likely to finish off their summer a few pounds heavier than when they started.

Readers may wonder why teams should be sent to such prosperous Christian countries at all. The sad fact is that underlying Scandinavia's immense wealth and beauty there exists a deep well of unbelief. Ninety per cent of the population are 'born Christians' inasmuch as they are automatic members of the state church. But only a very small minority recognise Jesus Christ as an important part of their daily lives. Less than 5 per cent attend church. Denmark and Sweden are the two most secular countries in Europe. As one team member in Sweden soberly observed, 'People just aren't interested in God here. I knew that before, but seeing it is different.'

But I have also seen that it is possible for internationally-mixed, highly-motivated Love Europe teams to catch the attention of people who have been inoculated against religion. Such teams may lack professional expertise, but the power of their personal testimonies coupled with their overflowing enthusiasm are undeniable. I remember one man in Berlin looking for a Love Europe team by inquiring for 'the people with the shining faces'. In Tidaholm, Sweden, we saw young people making an impact on local skinheads and gang members, largely through the testimony of a man from England who had himself been delivered from drugs and gambling.

In mid-July Tim, Linda and I, plus a campaign co-ordinator named Petra, took a ferry across the Gulf of Finland to Tallinn, Estonia. Friends had advised us that travel around the Baltics was best accomplished by train, so we left the car behind. This proved to be a major mistake right from the beginning. Erratic train connections meant that we wasted hours sitting around railway stations. In addition, the agent who sold us our Baltic train passes in Sweden neglected to inform us that we would be pioneering a new trail. Railroad personnel along the way received the passes with blank stares. We were obliged at each stop to go through endless explanations and checking with authorities before we were issued ongoing tickets.

In Tallinn we discovered we had six hours before the next train to Riga. It was Sunday, most things were closed and the weather had turned to a cold drizzle, but to kill time we took turns guarding the luggage and walking around. I had first seen this lovely medieval city four years before, when the country was on the verge of independence. Estonia, Latvia and Lithuania had been among the first republics to 'cry freedom' from Russia, and those of us who sailed to the Baltics aboard the OM ship *Logos II* in the summer of 1990 witnessed their euphoria. The Bibles and Christian books we carried were sold out immediately. Men, women and children turned toward God with the eager hunger of people who had long been deprived. I wondered now how much of that eagerness remained. The West had obviously made its impact. Tallinn's shop windows overflowed with Western products. Prices had also gone up considerably. I recalled the words of an Estonian friend with whom I corresponded: 'Our nation is hopelessly blinded with the sin of greed. Everyone is rushing and struggling with all their strength. There's no time to think of God, so we have not profitted much from freedom of religion.'

Back at the train station an inspection of the toilet facilities told me that at least one thing I remembered was unchanged. These particular toilets offered the usual hole in the floor, but at least it was relatively clean. To my consternation, however, a boisterous crowd of men trooped in while I was still trapped inside my cubicle. When I left they were all happily making use of the facilities without bothering to close any doors. I fled out to where the Russian attendant sat, but she only shrugged. Apparently the men's loo was closed; the woman saw no problem in collecting an admission charge wherever she could. A customer was a customer!

Eventually we boarded the overnight train to Riga and settled into our sleeping compartment. Sleep eluded me, not only because the train was swaying violently and making a racket but because there were four roaring drunks occupying the cabin next to us. At 2 or 3 a.m., when we crossed the Estonian-Latvian border, a succession of uniformed authorities pounded on the door every fifteen minutes to examine passports or tickets.

The first thing we did upon arrival in Riga was to secure ongoing tickets to Lithuania. This was no easy task since our English, and Petra's Swedish and Finnish, met only with shrugs. Eventually, however, a local person helped us obtain the precious permits and we made our way to Riga's Love Europe team.

We found the group quartered in an upper floor of a large, empty building, some of which was used as a school. They looked happy to see us but a quick survey dashed all hopes of a shower and comfortable sleep that night. Beds, baths and hot water did not exist at all, and toilets were primitive. But it was the stomach-turning smell that really grabbed our attention. For some reason the church that was hosting the team had stockpiled a massive heap of watermelons in the toilets. These had begun to rot in the intense heat and, to the team's dismay, the fruit was acting as a magnet to the local rat population. One of the rodents had reportedly crawled into a sleeping bag and another ran across the back of seventeen-year-old Carolyn Giles from England as she slept on the floor. Carolyn, surprisingly, considered it all a lark. 'It's been brilliant fun!' she exclaimed, laughing. 'The team spirit has been great! We blocked up the rat holes together and killed the cockroaches.' To crown their misfortunes the team's money had been stolen a few days before, while they were performing an open-air programme. I would have considered the young people worthy candidates for the summer's Scream Team award. They remained quite positive, however, believing that their tribulations had served to draw them together. Best of all, they said, they had been rewarded with seeing a number of Latvian and Russian citizens open their hearts to God's Good News.

Fifty years of Russian occupation and intermarriage left both Latvian and Estonian republics with a population that was roughly 30 to 40 per cent Russian. These transplanted Russians now regarded the Baltics as home. The problem was that for many older citizens, the trauma of the 1940 Soviet invasion – the murders and disappearances of loved ones – was neither forgiven nor forgotten. Ethnic hostility in the Baltic republics was still palpable. 'We didn't really understand the situation until we came here,' team leaders Christian and Lisette Gabre of Sweden confided. 'The feeling between Russians and Latvians exists even among Christians within the church. We were hurt to see it.' A Latvian translator added, 'Russians here feel like second class citizens. The team is a great testimony to people because of the different nationalities all getting along together.'

During the afternoon we joined the group distributing tracts, singing and performing drama in the city centre near the towering Freedom Monument. Translations were made into both Russian and Latvian languages. Although few spectators gathered to listen on this day, previous programmes had attracted audiences of between one and two hundred. Carolyn told me of an encounter she had had with an elderly Latvian who had spent time as a prisoner in Siberia. His wife had recently died, and the old man told her he wanted to jump out of a window and end it all. 'I just put my arms around him, and cried with him. I told him about Jesus. But you don't have all the answers. You just weep with them and pray for them.' All of the team agreed that a highlight of their Riga experience was the programme they held in a hospital. The children being treated in the facility were all victims of Chernobyl. 'I gave my testimony in German and someone translated into Russian and they all sat there listening to me,' one girl remembered. 'It was such a privilege. Afterwards I had a little girl in my lap and twenty more all around me, asking questions!'

By the time we got back to the school the stench of

decaying melons was unbearable. The rats had evidently been playing football in our absence for juice, seeds and pieces of rind lay everywhere. That did it. If the church would do nothing about the mess, we would have to clean it up ourselves. Tim organised a bag-and-bucket brigade and we spent the remainder of the afternoon hauling the sixty or seventy melons down four flights of steps to a rubbish dump outside. It wasn't the best solution for their disposal, perhaps, but at least the smell would no longer be under our noses. We then proceeded to wash down the whole area as best we could. In the process of searching for cleaning materials – scarce commodities in the Baltics – we opened all the kitchen cupboards and discovered cockroaches and rat droppings everywhere. Needless to say, we did not have hearty appetites for the remainder of our meals in Riga. And it was a long, long time before I could enjoy watermelon!

That night I unrolled my sleeping-bag onto a table-top, coward that I am, and lay alert for a long time. When the dreaded intruders failed to appear sheer tiredness dragged me into oblivion.

Fortunately our stay in Riga was a brief one. The next day we were on the train to Lithuania, reaching the city of Panevezys by early evening. The Love Europe team here was the first that OM had ever sent to this country, so we braced ourselves for the worst. We found the group staying in an old Russian apartment building which had been left largely vacant since the withdrawal of the military. Our discovery of a dead mouse and a dark, foul toilet in the rooms reserved for us made little impact after our last stop. There was even – glory be – a shower with plenty of hot water. Although this was located in a medieval cave in the cellar which had to be reached with a torch, we did not complain.

Some of the team were suffering stomach problems after drinking the tap water. We guessed that they had all struggled to adapt to the poverty. Residents could be seen sweeping the streets with bundles of sticks tied together, queueing up to exchange stacks of newspapers for toilet paper from a lorry, or fetching milk in their own containers. Water was often hand-pumped from central community wells. A car was an unthinkable luxury for most. The average teacher's salary, I was told, was about fifty dollars a month. 'I wouldn't want people here to see the house where I live and where my friends live,' confessed an American team member. 'They'd think we had palaces.' On the other hand, the committed lives of church people they'd met had left a deep impression. 'Christians here are so convinced about their faith. They really *live* as Christians! It's taught me not to be so concerned about myself.'

Joanne Reid from Australia let me read a diary entry describing a typical open-air programme they held in surrounding villages: 'When you invite people here there is no beating around the bush. You just tell them who you are and why you're here. I was astounded by how many came. They weren't like people in Australia; they seemed genuinely interested in what we had to say. I presented the "Wordless Book" and at the end of it about five prayed with me and accepted Christ. I couldn't believe my eyes! People in this country are looking for something to fill their empty lives.'

We spent one morning at an orphanage, singing songs and playing games and telling stories. I lost my heart to a little girl who clung to my hand and nestled close as we sat on the lawn. That afternoon the team visited patients in a local hospital. Our translators divided our group in half and told us we should only spend about ten minutes in each ward in order to cover them all. 'Ten minutes!' I was dismayed. 'What can we do in ten minutes?' Richard, our translator, smiled. 'You think we can't do anything? Wait. You'll see.' And so we did. Without exception, patients and their visitors in every room gave their full attention to our brief presentations. Many had tears in their eyes as they listened. A nurse wept openly. We answered their questions and prayed with those who requested it. Knowing that Lithuania is predominantly Catholic I tried to stress the importance of knowing the Lord on a personal level, not just mentally acknowledging his existence. A woman came to hug me joyfully after praying. 'I knew about Jesus in my head. Now I know Him in my heart!' We took down names and addresses for local pastors to follow up, but leaving those men and women, so eager and hopeful, was one of the hardest things I have ever had to do.

From Lithuania we caught another overnight train back to Estonia. Petra had to leave us because of other obligations, and Tim, Linda and I discovered that instead of getting a whole cabin to ourselves we'd been split up. Two were assigned to one compartment and the remaining one was alone in another. Both cabins were already occupied by half-naked men sprawled on the berths, with enough beer cans stockpiled between them to drink an army into oblivion. The Russian lady who was in charge of the section couldn't make head nor tail of our objections and left us standing obstinately in the corridor. After a while it dawned on us to look for a carriage with seats. Eureka! Linda and I found an unoccupied carriage and returned to collect Tim and the luggage. Jumping from one section of the swaying train to another, encumbered as we were, soon had us laughing hysterically. Finally we reached our destination and collapsed into the seats. But to our chagrin a scowling guard promptly descended upon us with a volley of Russian. It was clear that we weren't supposed to be there. Tim tried to mime out our situation. I thought his performance of a drunken man rather good but it failed to impress her. She disappeared and returned a few minutes later with reinforcements. Our hearts sank. We picked up our bags and staggered after the authorities, only to be brought up short at the entrance to an empty cabin. The guard motioned for us to go in. It was ours! We stared at each other incredulously. The staff had no doubt chalked us up as lunatics, but we didn't care.

Even with the multiple border checks that we passed through that night, we arrived at our destination at 5 a.m. the next morning deeply grateful for God's care. After buying a copy of a local paper, the *Baltic Observer*, our thankfulness increased: 'Overnight trains have become easy targets for criminals who lull passengers to sleep using, drugs or gas to steal their valuables,' we read. 'Police recorded 279 train robberies between Moscow and St Petersburg in the first six months of the year. Conductors advise passengers to tie a towel around compartment door handles to prevent break-ins.' Another newspaper bluntly commented: 'It would be better to give a Kalashnikov assault rifle to each section!'

The city of Tartu was the base for OM's permanent work in Estonia. Finnish team leaders Jyrki and Anna-Maija Raitila had moved to the republic in 1993 after leading several summer and Easter campaigns. I talked with Jyrki after breakfast and a much-needed shower in their home, and heard something of his vision for the country. With a population of only a million and a half, he believed it would be possible to give all Estonians the opportunity to respond to the gospel message by the year 2000. 'This means we want to provide a witness through literature, personal contact, and of course, churches. We see more and more that we should be helpers and encouragers of Estonians. They know how to evangelise, but they won't take the first step. Like Finns, they're naturally reserved. Russian oppression has also strangled initiative. That's why foreign campaigns like Love Europe are so important to get them going. All the Estonians involved in the past campaigns are still active, and those who were saved are still bearing fruit. Our prayer is that many Estonians will catch the mission vision for their own counry and beyond.'

Jyrki added that few Estonians were reaching out to Russians. Most churches were segregated, and the Estonian church was growing much faster. Tartu, in fact, still had no evangelical Russian church even though almost a third of its 115,000 population was Russian. It was apparent they were largely a forgotten people.

Fifty-one international men and women were involved in this summer's Love Estonia programme, along with an eighteen-voice Swedish youth choir that had proved extremely popular. We left Tartu to spend a few days with a team that was seeing a great response within a Russian area. Although they were sleeping on the floor of a church and only had their first shower after a week of hot weather, they were full of enthusiasm. 'In some places people were so happy to receive Bibles they brought us flowers or other gifts,' said Daniel Zeidan of Israel. 'Some of the Christians who saw us cried.'

I was encouraged to learn that there were still areas outside the larger cities where people were choosing to follow Jesus Christ. The Baltic capitals had been the focus of a bewildering parade of visiting evangelists and healers, cult followers and false teachers. Many had left behind a wake of confusion. For others the pursuit of the spiritual had been overtaken by a race for the material. It made me sad, but the battle for the Baltics was clearly not over.

My travelling companions and I went our separate ways in Tallinn. Tim and Linda were picking up the car in Finland and spending a few days with friends. I was taking the *Estonia* to Stockholm, where I would spend a final week with a Love Europe team. I remember that ferry trip best for the simple joys of a hot shower, clean toilets, and safe drinking-water. When I climbed into the clean sheets of my berth I fell deeply asleep, not waking until a cabinmate stepped on me on her way down from her bunk in the morning. On deck, though it was still very early the sky was bright, as it always is at that time of year in the Land of the Midnight Sun. I leaned against the rails, revelling in the beauty of the archipelago of islands around us. And then we docked in Stockholm.

Stockholm itself is built on islands, and in my opinion it is one of the loveliest of world capitals. The suburb of Rinkeby where I was heading was a different matter, however. Many Swedes don't like to acknowledge the existence of Rinkeby and most certainly won't set foot in it. Built originally to provide low-cost housing for large numbers of students and city employees, the tall blocks of flats gradually attracted more and more foreign workers. Today the square mile of Rinkeby houses approximately fourteen thousand people who speak a hundred different mother tongues.

Rinkeby International Church was started in 1989, largely through the efforts of ex-OMers. At the time of my visit the church offered fellowship groups in Arabic, Persian, English and Swedish. It was hoping eventually to conduct them in all ten of the major languages used in the area. In 1993 an OM team began working alongside the church, with Love Europe participants supplementing their efforts each summer. For missionaries-in-the-making, Rinkeby was the ideal place to get your feet wet! This summer, team leaders Matthias and Edna Pfleiderer had designed a questionnaire for campaigners to take from door to door. The survey was a useful way to introduce the community to the international church, and it also provided the church with valuable information. I was in time to accompany the team on their final night of survey-taking and was astonished at the range of nationalities we met. Living side by side in a single block were men and women from Iran, Iraq, Chile, Lithuania, Somalia, Ethiopia, and Nigeria! Even limited to speaking just English and some Spanish I was able converse with a number of them. All seemed friendly, polite, and pleased to receive the free video coupon we offered. Several showed a positive response toward visiting the church. I found out later that a number of them actually did.

The team's most dramatic door-to-door encounter happened just before I arrived. A woman had answered her door in her nightdress, perspiring and distraught, and invited the two team members inside. It was obvious that something was wrong and eventually Anne's story tumbled out: her depression over her father's death, her despair over a failed marriage and divorce. Anne confessed that she had already attempted once to take her life, but failed. She had been planning to try it again that night, when the doorbell rang. After talking with her for some time the girls urged Anne to attend the international church the following Sunday. She did so, and several weeks later this woman made up her mind to hand over her life to Jesus Christ.

Taking a day to explore Stockholm I discovered my bus and train pass included free admission to an open-air folk museum called Skansen. I wandered happily for hours through the re-created farm and village buildings, watching demonstrations of spinning and cheese-making. A zoo provided a close-up introduction to Sweden's four-footed inhabitants. Near to Skansen was the Vasa Museum, another not-to-be-missed stop for tourists. And of course, I could have spent days just browsing through the shops lining the narrow lanes of the old city. I stress the word 'browsing' for Swedish products are as costly as they are beautiful!

Stockholm was the end-of-season departure point for several dozen Love Europe teams. On the scene to gather their stories, I watched vans and buses pour into a local church and offload exhausted but excited members of 'the mustard seed conspiracy'. The young people couldn't wait to throw their arms around old friends and relate their adventures. The Murmansk, Russia, team had taken an arduous four days to get to Sweden. 'The Russian church worked us to death!' they cried dramatically, but added, 'We had an incredible time!' An American girl fell upon her breakfast of cornflakes with glee. 'I'm so sick of Russian bread! It took hours to chew it!' A German participant glowed as she told me about the children she had met in Estonia who had decided to 'live with Jesus'. A group staggering in from Gdansk, Poland, headed straight for the showers. They had been introducing people to the Lord through English classes. Some announced they were already planning on going back next year.

. . . Next year . . . We take so much for granted! I left Stockholm and returned to London a few days later. Weeks after my own voyage aboard the *Estonia* from Tallinn to Stockholm, the ferry's loading door was accidentally left open when she left port. The *Estonia* sank to the bottom of the Baltic Sea carrying nine hundred men, women and children to their deaths.

It's the sort of thing that makes you stop and think.

11

Down to the sea again

In November 1994 OM's two ships, the *Doulos* and *Logos II*, berthed together for the first time. The event took place in the French port of Toulon to mark the twenty-fifth year of the ships' ministry, and friends and ex-crew members from all over the world joined the 'On Course' celebrations. Those of us who travelled from London chartered a double-decker. As we came to the end of the twenty-four hour journey we looked eagerly for our first glimpse of the ships' familiar white funnels. The moment carried a strong sense of *déjà vu*. Nine years before I had been a new recruit arriving by coach to join the *Doulos* in Naples, Italy. My feelings then had oscillated between excitement and trepidation. This time I climbed the *Doulos* gangway with a sense of coming home. I would be sailing with her for the next two months, writing articles about the ship and her crew.

Oddly enough, my assigned cabin was right next door to the one I'd occupied years before. Number 237 was about as far below deck as you can get on the starboard side. It was also cocooned in an interior section, which meant there were no portholes and all lighting was artificial. I recalled a Korean family in the old days who had insisted on plugging in their rice cooker every Saturday. Invariably,

the fuses blew and we were all plunged into total darkness –
a particularly trying situation if one happened to be caught
in the shower.

Like all cabins, my new home was compact. Besides two
narrow bunks it contained a four-drawer chest of drawers,
plus two narrow clothes lockers. The space in the latter
was seriously limited by the bulky lifejackets they also had
to accommodate. A strip of flooring beside the bunks was
just large enough to allow one person at a time to dress
or undress. I was allocated the top berth. A Filipino girl
was already occupying the lower one. Luz had spread her
possessions over every inch of available space but upon my
arrival she obligingly consolidated everything. In a few more
weeks, she assured me, she would be finishing her three-year
commitment and returning home for a break. Sleeping on
the top bunk was no problem, once you'd mastered the art
of vaulting up and down via the dresser top (the manoeuvre
was a bit trickier to negotiate when the ship was at sea). I
didn't plan to be spending much time in my quarters anyway.
The real challenge was finding a quiet corner where I could
plug in my laptop. The photo lab/printshop crew cheerfully
came to my rescue. I shared their workspace for the first
few weeks and later transferred to a vacant desk in one of
the offices. On a ship, no space goes unoccupied for long.

The first week I was absorbed into the whirlwind of 'On
Course' events. The first guest weekend drew 500 friends.
Three hundred and twenty German prayer–partners came
later the same week, followed by 530 Swiss. For many
visitors it was their first chance to see both or even one
of the ships. The atmosphere was charged with emotional
reunions between old shipmates. I wasn't the only one
scrabbling desperately to put names to faces, and trying
to recall on which of the three ships and in what year we'd

been together! The happiest reunion was with my old friend, Susie Burton. She had been back serving as the *Doulos* photographer for the last year and we looked forward to working together again during the next two months. From a reporter's point of view there simply wasn't enough time to capture all the good stories that there were in Toulon. However, the week was remarkably rewarding, and each one who came undoubtedly returned to their homes with a renewed enthusiasm to support 'God's navy.'

A number of reunion visitors flew in and out of Nice. When Susie volunteered to drive a couple to the airport in one of the ship's vans, she invited a half-dozen of us who had the day off to go along too. We packed a picnic lunch (with the help of a galley-worker who had strategically been included in the invitation), and after depositing the airport passengers we continued a half-hour up the coast to Monte Carlo. The French Riviera! We gaped like country yokels at the elegance of the palazzos scattered along the hillsides, the yachts anchored in an aquamarine sea. Eventually we stopped on a stretch of beach to eat our sandwiches and I wandered along the shore. Who knew whether I might stumble across a lost diamond necklace, or a lonely millionaire? This was not to be my fate, alas, but it was fun to explore the playground of the rich! A few of our number boldly went inside the most famous casino – only to use the loo, of course. They emerged in amazement. A New Zealand friend and I tried the Hotel de Paris next door, but we were turned away by snobbish doormen. Must have been the scruffy shoes.

During our last days in Toulon a container of stores was delivered to the *Doulos* quayside. All available hands were called to pass cartons and sacks up to the lift on board, and I found a place in the chain next to the director's wife.

The hard work was lightened by laughter and a running commentary on the goods passing through. There were predictable cheers from the British and groans from the Americans when the Marmite appeared. Crates of peanut butter triggered just the opposite response. When a box of noodles broke on the gangway and tumbled into the water, a couple of Asian men went to heroic lengths to rescue the floating packages. Large cartons of tins were the real back-breakers. For the next couple of days I paid for overestimating my stevedore strength!

On the morning of 22 November, the crews of both the *Logos II* and *Doulos* met for the last time. The weeks together had forged a strong spirit of unity that was reflected by the various crew members who spoke. The devotional challenge was followed by hasty farewell hugs and photo-taking, and then it was time to draw up the gangways. A lively debate over which one of our ships should lead the way from the harbour was amicably settled: Both parties agreed that the 'Word' – *Logos* – should rightfully precede the 'Servant' – *Doulos*. However, I'm afraid that we on the *Doulos* forgot our humility when we got into open water: our ship pulled alongside and then steamed ahead. Everyone on both ships lined the rails, waving and cheering hysterically. I stood on the bridge brandishing a hastily painted message: '*Vaya Con Díos*, Little Sister!' Then we slipped further and further apart, the *Logos II* heading west to Spain, while we turned east towards Italy. I felt torn, wishing somehow I could be on both ships at once. When and where would our two vessels meet again?

Early the next morning we slipped into the beautiful harbour of La Spezia. Now that we were in Italy I felt as though I had truly come full circle, although it was Naples and not this northern port where I had first joined OM's ship ministry. We learned that because of her size the *Doulos* would have to be berthed stern-end in to the quayside. It was an awkward position, but the Italian Navy obligingly loaned us pontoon floats to serve as a walkway alongside the port side, so we could use our gangways. The greatest problem was how to offload our vans, which were parked near the bow. The deck crew came up with the ingenious idea of lowering each vehicle onto a sturdy raft via the ship's derrick. The raft was then floated to the quayside where another crane lifted each van onto the road. Everyone heaved a sigh of relief when the vans all made their precarious voyage without mishap.

Thanksgiving happened to coincide with our arrival, a day the Americans were not about to let pass without a proper observance. Thanks to the connivance of a Yankee cook and several others we were able to come up with a real old-fashioned feast. The Canadians were magnanimously invited to join us. Their Thanksgiving officially fell on a different date, but they weren't inclined to make an issue of it. We sat together in the forward section of the dining-room that was decorated with Canadian and American flags. After a few traditional songs and prayer we dug into the turkey, potato and cranberry sauce with a true spirit of appreciation. The rest of the crew were not so appreciative, but we hardened our hearts.

Our *Doulos* Thanksgiving Day did not quite stretch to parades and football games, however – the ship's official opening for La Spezia was scheduled for the afternoon. Officers hurried to don their uniforms and those of us with assigned duties put on our Sunday best. The reception was to be graced by the Prefect of La Spezia and other VIPs, so it was essential for all to go well. My job was to assist with a press conference and conduct the media around the ship. An Italian national TV crew, in fact, spent five hours recording a five-minute news segment about the *Doulos*. Everyone seemed interested in the fact that *Doulos* had once belonged to the Italian Costa Line of cruise ships. When Nicolas Costa, the present director, later paid us a brief visit, leaders presented him with two old paintings that used to hang in the lounge for the Costa Line Museum. Seventy students from La Spezia's Nautical School were also interested in touring our vessel as the *Doulos* was designated by the *Guinness Book of Records* as the oldest sea-going passenger ship in the world. During a special programme for them, the young seamen received a challenge by Chief Engineer Rex Worth to consider sailing with Jesus Christ. Four 'Operation World' conferences that took place in La Spezia encouraged over eleven hundred Italian Christians to spread their nets of concern to the rest of the world.

My cabin-mate departed for the Philippines on the first Saturday in port. I accompanied Luz to the Pisa airport and afterwards got my first glimpse of the famous Leaning Tower. Seeing this tourist attraction in real life was more amazing than I expected. The bell-tower is a beautiful structure on its own, as ornate as a wedding cake, but it should really be viewed in relation to the nearby cathedral and baptistry. Visitors used to be able to climb the tower but it is now deemed unsafe. I was content just to stand in front of this extraordinary architectural 'accident', that has claimed so much attention.

As much as I would miss the cheerful companionship of Luz, I had to admit that I had been gleefully anticipating the extra space. The cabin could even provide me with another workplace. Alas, those dreams evaporated as soon as I returned from Pisa. A frantic leader rushed up to tell me that half a dozen extra Italian volunteers had shown up unexpectedly. The young people had come a long distance to serve two weeks on the ship. Could one of the girls use the empty bed in my cabin? I sighed; of course there was no question of refusing. The bed and the cabin belonged to God, like the ship itself. Besides, the arrangement was only supposed to last two weeks (although I was convinced that some other emergency would crop up by the end of it). At least, however, I could shift to the lower bunk. My new cabin-mate didn't speak any English but we got on very well, especially since we rarely laid eyes on each other. Sometimes late at night or early in the morning, before I got up, I was sure I heard two voices in the adjoining toilet. This puzzled me for days until Ester finally explained that another volunteer friend was sharing a cabin with three other girls. Since it was difficult for her to get time in the bathroom she came over to use mine!

Several teams left the ship to work with small churches in Sardinia and other parts of Italy. Susie and I decided to invite ourselves along with a group heading for the hills of Tuscany with a rather unusual assignment. The Ammirables were a Christian family who had done a lot to promote the *Doulos* visit in Italy. Now Giovanni, the head of the family, was in urgent need of hands to bring in his olive harvest. So Susie and I got some great pictures and stories of an olive-picking team! Of course we also got in on the action ourselves, climbing ladders to rake the hard green fruit from the highest branches. I felt a little as though I was raking blueberries back in Maine! The family kept up their crew's strength with plenty of pasta, olives and hunks of bread and cheese; no doubt the team wished they could stay for ever.

Susie and I left first, but before catching our train from Florence to La Spezia we squeezed in a memorable few hours of sightseeing. Who could do anything but marvel at the Piazza Vecchio, the Piazzale Michelangelo, the Cathedral, the narrow streets lined with elegant shops decorated for Christmas? We paused to treat ourselves to a cappuccino near the Ponte Vecchio. Longfellow's *The Old Bridge At Florence* still gives the best description of the famous bridge:

> ... I am old; five centuries old. I plan my foot of stone upon the Arno ... Florence adorns me with her jewellery. And when I think that Michael Angelo hath leaned on me, I glory in myself.

The jewellery in the very exclusive shops along the bridge would never adorn Susie or me, but who cared? We too had been able to lean upon the same stone as Michelangelo!

Before we knew it our two weeks in Italy were up. On the last morning everyone who was free took the traditional hike into town to spend their remaining pocket money. The fact that we each had only a few lira made the great decision all the more critical. Most of my companions opted for Italian ice cream, postcards, or chocolate, but after half an hour of hanging over the many gorgeous varieties of flowers in the open market, I finally chose a potted poinsettia. The huge bloom would do wonders in brightening my cabin. And after all, Christmas was only a few weeks away!

Christmas is one of my favourite times of year. I'd been careful to pack decorations when I knew I'd be spending this year's holiday on the ship. And since snow often comes along the same time in my native New England, I devoted spare moments to creating tissue snowflakes. Whoever descended to our accommodation section in the ship found themselves in the midst of a veritable blizzard. Regretfully, the Greek vessel *Achille Lauro* was burned to the water line about that time somewhere else in the Mediterreanean, and everyone became very safety conscious. When Captain O'Reilly came upon my snowflakes during an inspection he ordered them all removed from the bulkheads. Afterwards the captain made a point of apologising. I thought that sweet of him – but I did mourn the loss of my winter wonderland!

12

Change of course

Sailing into Malta's Grand Harbour that December I relived the thrill of my first visit seven years before. The limestone battlements and sun-drenched parapets rose around us with the same ageless dignity. The harbour might have been built as a medieval film set – in fact, an adventure tale was being shot directly across from our berth.

The historic ambience inspired a friend and I to invest our precious pocket money in seeing the multi-screen 'Maltese Experience'. The presentation gave us a tremendous respect for the island and its people. I was particularly impressed at how Malta had stood as the last Allied outpost between Europe and North Africa during World War Two. After their homes were pounded nearly into oblivion by German bombers, residents took shelter in caves. They nearly starved when ships failed to break through the blockade, yet somehow they managed to hang on – and in doing so they won the admiration of the world.

The Maltese have shown the same tenaciousness in their faith. Roman Catholic churches crowd the island and are faithfully packed to the doors for mass. Statues of the saints are everywhere, staring down somberly from buildings and roadside shrines. The island in fact enjoys a reputation as the jewel in the Pope's crown with almost every family having contributed a nun or priest to missionary service. For many years, marriages weren't even recognised outside the Catholic Church; dissenting couples were obliged to travel-to England for the ceremony. The Protestant Church only gained a foothold through British troops stationed there. Malta's evangelical community numbered only about a hundred until the mid-eighties. At the time of our visit ten years on, the *Doulos* was welcomed by nine churches with over four hundred members. On our first Sunday evening they gathered in the ship's lounge for a joyful celebration.

The visit of our 'bookship' was also warmly endorsed by Malta's government. At an official reception, President Ugo Bonnici declared the *Doulos* was 'probably the best means for spreading peace; a carrier of knowledge and a work done out of love, for which the world must be thankful'. Captain Michael O'Reilly and Director George Barathan were careful to credit the spirit of peace and unity on board to our spiritual Captain, Jesus Christ. The guests at the reception were happy to take home complimentary copies of the *Jesus* video.

Doulos men were always keen to get some exercise so when a local rugby team proposed a match, the invitation was readily accepted. Our men thought they were agreeing to a friendly game of touch rugby. Imagine their horror when they turned up in T-shirts and trainers at the appointed hour, and found themselves facing Malta's national champions! Their hefty opponents were decked out in full uniform with studded boots, armoured and ready for a full contact match! It was clearly a case of David versus Goliath. The temptation to retreat was strong but pride came to the rescue. The Maltese generously loaned our men five players to make up the necessary numbers, but both teams had little doubt as to how things would turn out. It's debatable which side was more stunned when the game finished with a two point victory – for the *Doulos*! The crew members who participated limped around painfully for several days but they wore their bruises as badges of honour. They should have remembered that pride comes before a fall. Later that same week another dozen of our men accepted an invitation to play basketball. Our team was soundly trounced, with a score too humiliating to repeat.

My own challenge in Malta wasn't quite so athletic. I was scheduled to teach a three-hour introductory writing workshop as part of the on-board programme. Considering the size of the island and the specialised nature of my subject I was content when fifteen turned up. They were a mixed bag of housewives, students, pastors, a retired doctor/politician, and one or two people from the ship; but each person came keen to learn.

At the close of our session Leo, one of the crew members, escorted the doctor on a tour of the ship. He was surprised to learn the doctor had once served as a leader of Malta's Labour party, and Speaker of the Parliament. At one point the man had even held the fort as acting president for eleven days. A week after the workshop, the doctor invited Leo and a few friends to visit him in his home. The house turned out to be an enormous and imposing palazzo in Mdina. Leo couldn't wait to tell me afterwards that when they went into the library he saw the doctor's desk covered with notes from the writing workshop. And lying among the notes was an open New Testament. I recalled then that during our time together we had discussed various motivations for writing. The disciple John had stated his purpose clearly, and I quoted his words: 'These [things] are written that you may believe that Jesus is the Christ, the

Son of God, and that by believing you may have life in his name' (John 20:31). Could this be the verse the old doctor had been studying? The man made no claim of following Jesus Christ, but perhaps John's forthright statement had challenged him. I hoped that he would explore further in the Book of Books, and decide the truth for himself.

As the sailing date of 20 December drew closer our anxiety increased. The next port of call was supposed to be Tunisia, but line-up personnel still hadn't secured a definite confirmation from the country's government. It was only on the eve of sailing that we got the news: permission was denied. Tunisian officials told our representatives that the timing of our proposed visit was not convenient. The cancellation was a tremendous disappointment to everyone. My own decision to sail with the *Doulos* instead of the *Logos II* had, in fact, been largely based on the plan to spend Christmas in Tunis. The event would have been history-making, bringing more Christians to that city in one time than it had seen for thirteen centuries. So why hadn't God chosen to overrule?

Leaders made the decision to stay in Malta an extra week. Unfortunately we had to give up our excellent berth and move across the harbour to a grain-loading dock that was too dangerous to allow public access. The book exhibition had to be closed. And Valletta was now too far to reach on foot. Outreach activities, which had not really received much response from the Maltese anyway, were now more difficult to arrange. But we decided to make the most of what opportunities we had.

'Twas the day before Christmas, and all through the ship . . . every creature was stirring! I was determined not to miss anything, so when a drama team went to Valletta on the morning of 24 December I tagged along. The narrow streets were jammed with last-minute shoppers. We made our way to the central square where a stage had been erected to provide a continuous supply of holiday entertainment. Our group was to perform a twenty-minute mime called 'A Tale of Two Kingdoms'. The play is about a prince who leaves his father's kingdom in order to redeem his captive subjects. Although the story unravels as a fairy tale, the gospel message is powerfully implicit. So it was easy, when the drama finished, to engage bystanders in conversations about what they'd seen.

I wasn't present for the second performance. I wish I had been. When the actors left the stage, ship evangelist Ray Lentzsch stepped out to invite the audience to respond to God's great gift of his Son. About twenty-five well-dressed Maltese responded. Unashamed to declare their gratitude and their need of a Saviour, they moved from the crowd and knelt in the public square. A scene like that isn't often seen in Malta – or anywhere else in sophisticated society, for that matter. Ray was more aware of that fact than most people. Thirty years before he had preached the same message in almost the identical spot, opposite Valletta's Courts of Justice, and been arrested for it. During the next ten years of winters in Malta, Ray saw only a handful of men and women make a personal commitment to follow Christ. How like our God not only to allow Ray the joy of being present on this Christmas Eve 1994 – but to use him to help bring about an extraordinary breakthrough!

At the same time, in another part of Malta, I was part of another group who were visiting the national prison. The building was old and grim, the kind of place that creates instant depression. Our team was ordered to hold our programme in the 'Protestant chapel', which guaranteed that all the Catholic Maltese inmates would not attend.

That left an audience of about ten foreigners from Ghana, Liberia, Nigeria and Tanzania, plus one lone Italian. Most of the Africans professed faith in Jesus Christ and were grateful for any diversion from their dreary incarceration. They entered into the singing and worship with gusto. The young Italian wasn't a believer nor did he speak English, but fortunately we had an Italian shipmate with us. Raffaele spoke with this inmate for a long while, and learned that God had already been at work in his past. The man was ready to make this Christmas Eve the turning-point and confessed his need of a Saviour. Afterwards, as we distributed the biscuits, chocolate and greetings cards we had brought with us for the prisoners, it seemed to me a true celebration, in spite of the surroundings. A birthday gift to bring a smile to the King.

But this remarkable day was not yet over. The sailors of the good ship *Doulos* cast off for their own Christmas Eve festivities for the rest of the evening, with groups meeting by nationality to enjoy their own traditional food, games and singing. Countries represented by very small numbers (we had only a single Egyptian, one Albanian and four Mongolians) joined with other national groups. I know the Swiss had a good time because they used the cabin next to mine and devoured cheese fondue! We thirty or so Americans brought so many goodies we had to fend off would-be poachers from South Africa, Holland and Korea. We were also required to bring a white elephant 'gift' from our cabins for a Yankee swap. During this rather hectic exercise, participants could either choose a wrapped-up present or confiscate an item someone else had already unwrapped. I was doing pretty well with a packet of biscuits until someone spotted them. Alas, Santa left me with the grand prize of a razor!

When the refreshments and games were over we sang carols. Old favourites like 'White Christmas' and 'I'll Be Home For Christmas' provoked the inevitable sentimentality – there wasn't one of us who didn't miss loved ones from back home. But judging by the festivity that rocked our boat that Christmas Eve, being a member of God's family brought its own special rewards.

Before we hit our bunks, a few hundred of us tip-toed around playing Father Christmas, sticking home-made cards and little gifts on cabin doors. Gift-giving on a ship full of volunteers is a humble affair. A chocolate bar or sweet might be equivalent to a whole box of chocolates given in normal circumstances. But each gift was all the more cherished for the sacrifice in pocket money it represented. Christmas also gave us a chance to leave little tokens of appreciation for the hard-working laundry girls, the cleaning team, and others. The gangway watchmen came in for their share of treats from me. I always felt so sorry for the men assigned to stand the long, tedious, and often cold night watches while the rest of us were tucked snugly in our bunks.

On Christmas morning we all gathered in the lounge to honour the One who united all of our nationalities, our King of Kings. Young people from the small mission ship *Redeemer*, berthed close by, also joined us for the day. The *Redeemer* was part of a ministry called Seacare, and was run by a couple who had served with OM's first ship, the *Logos*. The *Redeemer* had sustained some damage and needed a number of repair jobs doing, so *Doulos* deckmen and engineers had been volunteering extra work hours to get her back into running condition.

Christmas dinner was a real labour of love, beautifully prepared and served by the galley staff. No passengers on a luxury cruise liner could have eaten better than we did. And that evening we had another Christmas-around-the-World celebration, featuring an entertaining variety of songs and skits. On Boxing Day the ship's children presented their nativity play, and after that things went back more or less to normal. The decision had been made to sail for Cyprus on 27 December. A few hours before we cast off, my friend Susie Burton disembarked with a number of other crew members who had fulfilled their commitments. Susie planned a detour to Tunisia to take photos before returning to New Zealand, where she meant to start up her own photography business. Goodbyes were difficult. We had parted from each other so many times before, never knowing if we would ever meet again. This time the separation looked to be permanent.

The pilot boat escorted our ship out of Grand Harbour on a bright, windy afternoon. As she left with a blast of her horn, a motorised raft suddenly appeared from nowhere. The little craft bounced wildly over the waves in pursuit of our vessel, filled to capacity with cheering, waving passengers whom we finally recognised as our friends from the *Redeemer*. It was a heartwarming farewell.

I enjoyed every moment of our three-day sail to Cyprus. When I wasn't on deck, soaking in the majesty of the passing islands, the wind and sea, I was button-holing anyone who might provide an interesting story. Unfortunately all of the work departments were understaffed. The ship's complement of 350 people had fallen to an unprecedented 275 – a situation I hoped to do something about. To my way of thinking, no Christian with an ounce of adventure in their blood would refuse a stint in God's Navy, if only they knew what it was like! Where else could you rub shoulders with so many fascinating people? I listened with awe to Malaysian William Koo, who told me how he had been dedicated to a Buddhist god when he was a baby, and how his quest for truth led to the one true God. Kathrin Weyermann, a trained housekeeper from Switzerland, regaled me with dozens of hilarious anecdotes of her behind-the-scenes job as supervisor of the *Doulos* accommodation team. And Ankie Romeijn from the Netherlands took me through the trauma of the Philippine grenade attack on the crew back in 1990.

One of the most riveting stories came from Rebekah Mugarenang. Rebekah had left Papua New Guinea and joined the *Doulos* for unique reason: to fill the gap left by the death of a white missionary who was murdered – and eaten – by her own great-grandfather! Rebekah's grandfather was only a boy at the time but he had refused to take part in the feast. He started attending a mission school and it was there he became a committed Christian. Rebekah attributed her own faith largely to him.

Men and women came to the *Doulos* from all sorts of professions: graphic design, education, mechanics, medicine. The previous May, nurses and doctors on board had been unexpectedly called upon to meet an emergency in the Red Sea. The ship had been on its way to the Suez Canal when the radio officer intercepted an SOS call: an Egyptian ferry was on fire and sinking with 588 passengers. A United States naval vessel in the area co-ordinating the rescue asked for all possible medical assistance. The *Doulos* reversed its course and sent three doctors, twelve nurses, and five Arabic translators to the American ship. It also just 'happened' that the *Doulos* had been given a number of intravenous drips which were needed for treating victims. The US radio officer commented, 'Your ship and medical team have been an absolute godsend.' An official letter of thanks was later sent from the Commander of the US Department of the Navy's Middle East Force.

The *Doulos* tied up in Limassol on the last day of 1994. After receiving orientation that evening, the crew began to reflect on the ways God had steered his ship through the nineteen ports of the past year. Just before midnight I slipped out on deck. The sky above the harbour was disappointingly dark, but a German shipmate turned up that moment, triumphantly flourishing a handful of sparklers sent from home. Enlisting the Finnish watchman's help we ran down the gangway and lit our miniature fireworks against the night. Like children, we laughed and shouted and paraded our flares along the quayside. By the time we trooped in to join the rest of the crew, they were already making inroads on great quantities of ice cream and doughnuts. The New Year had begun!

The *Doulos* had just left an island of strategic importance. We were now on another such island. Cyprus's position in the Mediterranean and its comparative freedom of religion made it a logical launchpad to the entire Middle East. If we had any doubts on that score, they were dispelled by the number of mission personnel who welcomed us to Cyprus. The unexpected visit by the *Doulos* was not only an encouragment to the island's small evangelical community; it gave ship staff an important insight into the work going on in nearby countries. To the other mission agencies, our crew members were potential recruits.

I was delighted to meet up with friends from my former mission, Christian Literature Crusade. The Argyrides family had also transferred from CLC and now served with AMG International in Larnaca. On the first Sunday in port I accompanied a team to their church and went home with them for lunch. Stathis and Carolynn now had three children. Emily, only three when I last saw her, had blossomed into a teenager. Her brother Solomon had been born with Downs Syndrome just after the family came to Cyprus. And in 1993, the Argyrides made history by becoming the first people to adopt a Cypriot child with Downs. Little Fanouris was proving to be a loving playmate for Solomon.

Since the decision to stop in Cyprus had been made at the last minute, the ship preparation team had had only three days to secure permissions and publicise a programme. They did a remarkable job. Over ten thousand visitors came up the gangways in just ten days; the profits from the books that they purchased were enough to pay for the ship's forthcoming passage through the Suez Canal. As Acting Director George Barathan told me on the day I left, perhaps the Cyprus visit had been one of God's reasons for overruling Tunisia at that time.

I had delayed my return to London as long as I could. In a few more days the *Doulos* would be setting out again, down through the Red Sea to India. On 8 January, with regret, I closed the door of my little cabin for the last time and went down the gangway, escorted by my shipmates. I felt I had added very little to their lives compared to the contributions they had made to mine. No longer strangers, these young people were the newest members of my ever-increasing, international family.

13

Before the gods

As soon as I got home in January I began working hard to finish the stories I'd drafted while on the ships, before the next big trip, scheduled for 1 March. Like most people I write best when events are still fresh in my mind. Besides, magazine editors could take months to decide if they wanted a piece. If they sent it back with a rejection slip I would have to start the submission process all over again. And with some articles, the time element was critical. But when Philip Morris told me he urgently needed material for his department's magazine *India Today*, and would underwrite the expense of a two-week assignment, it was too good an offer to refuse. I hadn't been to India for about five years. It was time to go back and feel the pulse of the subcontinent.

I left on a cold February morning for a twenty-four-hour flight that would include a stop-over in Kuwait. Kuwait Airlines was not, it appeared, over-concerned with passengers' requests. A number of us found ourselves seated in the smoking section after specifically asking to be in no-smoking. A man across the aisle lit up as soon as we were airborne, but the plane was packed and there was no possibility of changing seats. I tried to forget my discomfort with the book I'd brought along, but this also proved a problem. 'Can you do something about this blinking light?' I finally asked the flight attendant. I wasn't being rude, the overhead reading light *was* blinking. The attendant shrugged helplessly, so a black-swathed Muslim lady at the window took matters into her own hands and blocked off the light completely with a piece of paper. That didn't help my reading at all, but not wishing to offend I said nothing. While she dozed I played a game of Uno with the young Kuwaiti boy beside me who had been wistfully shuffling his pack of cards.

Eventually I made my way down to the toilets, stepping over a man kneeling on his prayer mat. His sense of direction was far more acute than mine if he was sure which way to face for Mecca. In the toilet I noted regretfully that the complimentary toothbrushes had already been used up. I tried the skin-freshener and wasted as much time as possible before returning to my seat. Still no signs of a meal being served, so I dug up the biscuits and M&Ms I'd brought along for emergencies. As soon as I'd finished them the attendants wheeled their food trollies down the aisles. Oh, well. I managed to finish off my tray anyway. You had to seize every opportunity when you couldn't be sure where the next meal was coming from – or what it might be like!

Fortunately the inflight movie, *The Client*, was one I hadn't seen before and it successfully diverted me from thoughts of mid-air collisions for the rest of the stretch to Kuwait. Unfortunately we touched down at a critical moment, ten minutes before the film ended. I was tempted to ask an attendant about the fate of the protagonist but they were all preoccupied.

My first stop in the airport toilets reminded me that I

was indeed in the Middle East. Good thing I remembered the cardinal rule of travel: BYOTP (Bring Your Own Toilet Paper)! I whiled away the four-hour stop-over looking in the windows of expensive shops. When that palled I was entertained by the sight of sheikhs sweeping by in flowing white, their wives flocking behind like black crows. Why were the oldest ladies the most assiduous in veiling their faces from the lustful gaze of men, when they were the least in need of it?!

The shining elegance of the airport was meant to impress, and it did. The discovery of 'black gold' had turned a desert oasis into one of the richest countries in the world. But wealth attracts envy, and neighbouring Iraq had attempted to get a piece of it. What had Kuwait City been like with the Gulf War turning normal life upside down, I wondered, when Muslim brother had warred against Muslim brother and 'Christian' nations had to come to the rescue? Kuwait had spent a lot of its oil money on defeating Christianity, buying Bibles to burn and rewarding those who converted to Islam. What now?

Even if I could have afforded to buy anything I had no space to carry it. I had packed with extraordinary economy on this trip: only an overnight bag to check in and a shoulder-bag containing camera, toiletries, some emergency food (already depleted) and drinking water. But I worried about my check-in: I'd locked the main compartment but the two side-pockets were vulnerable. The last time I checked in a similar holdall, going to Hong Kong, the pockets got rifled and I lost all the earrings I'd accumulated since the *Logos* shipwreck.

Dawn was just breaking when we spanned the last stretch of our trip and dropped down into Bombay. Somewhere since the previous morning I had lost five and a half hours, and there were miles to go yet before I would be able to sleep. A shuttle bus transferred me to the domestic airport where I sat sleepily awaiting the 9.30 a.m. flight south to Cochin, swatting mosquitoes that evidently found me to their taste. Hopefully my malaria tablets would work.

For the following hour and a half that I spent in the air I sat glued to the window, totally absorbed by the changing panorama below. As we moved from north to south, the subcontinent became noticeably richer and greener. The thick jungles of palm trees might have been mistaken for my native evergreens until we dropped low enough to see them clearly. But stepping from the plane into the steamy heat of the tropics removed all doubt about where I was. It was 28°C, and this wasn't even summertime!

Two girls were awaiting my arrival with smiles and we took a three-wheeled cab, called an auto-rickshaw, to their team's flat. OM's Love India programme had been launched to give young people from around the world an effective short-term mission experience. Focusing on middle-class, English-speaking Hindus and Muslims meant that foreigners didn't have to learn another language during their six months in India. Also, living conditions in middle-class neighbourhoods required less of an adjustment. Those who joined one of the all-men's or all-women's teams experienced the culture close up, and were plunged head first into a variety of outreach opportunities.

The women on the Cochin team came from Germany, Switzerland, the Netherlands and England, as well as India. Their flat was the upper floor of a large and airy house surrounded by tall coconut palms, mango trees and hibiscus. Although everyone slept on mats on the floor, the facilities included both Western-style and Asian toilets. That cheered me considerably. So did the shower, although I took rather less pleasure in it after the girls warned me about the giant spiders. These were apparently harmless enough, but they had a bad habit of jumping on people. The ants I didn't mind so much, although they trailed their way over everything I put on the window sill or floor.

The team held a Women's Bible study for new believers and contacts on my first afternoon. I could scarcely keep my eyes open but it seemed too important to miss. When I finally did succumb I slept like a log for the first four or five hours. Then I woke up burning and itching all over – mosquitos were eating me alive! The rest of the night I managed only intermittent sleep, battling both my unseen predators and the heat, which was too oppressive for even a sheet. Next morning the girls promised me they'd find a mosquito net.

Since it was Sunday we took a bus to go to the Cochin Faith Assembly. The church turned out to be a tiny cement room on a rooftop jammed with benches and far too many bodies. I was feeling strangely dizzy as I sat there, no doubt dehydrated. Even so my eyes opened wider at some of the English songs written on the overhead. 'There is power in the blood of the lamp' was surely meant to be *Lamb*, I mused; and 'Abiding in the wine' was a striking thought, but a trifle less biblical than abiding in the vine. Some of the girls on the team who were nearing the end of their six-month commitment were asked to share their testimonies. I listened with interest, and learned more later as I talked with them individually.

Jo Sheldon had finished teacher training back in England and decided to travel before settling to work. 'When I first came to India I loved the vibrance, the colour. I was pretty high – for a week! And then I faced the reality. But I've learned so much more through Love India than I would have as a tourist. It's been brilliant! I've taught Bible studies and English lessons, visited door-to-door, done children's work in local slums, schools, and orphanages. Once we went bathing in the Arabian Sea – fully clothed, of course! And I had only one case of "Delhi belly". It hasn't always been easy of course. I've never really been so apart from my culture. But I'm glad I didn't stay in my Western bubble. At home I never appreciated the difference between my God and the gods the Hindus worship – I took him for granted.'

Bianca Weiermuller of Stuttgart, Germany confessed that she faced a crisis in her faith after joining the team. 'The first thing I saw coming into Bombay was a big slum. I thought, "What have I done?!" There were so many beggars, the dust and dirt were overwhelming. I wondered how I could ever cope. On the team I started to read the Bible more, and it spoke to me. I feel the world is much smaller now. I have much more motivation to pray, and much more understanding of other cultures. Joining Love India is like walking on ice – you have to trust God to hold you up!'

The three Indian girls on the team had their own share of adjustments to make. They were often called upon to bridge the gaps for the newcomers, yet they too struggled with the local language and customs since they were from different parts of India. Neisau, from Nagaland in the extreme north-east, said even the food was different. But according to team leader Beena Jose, the idea of putting national and international women together was proving effective. Not only did they learn from each other, but the very fact that they *were* living and working together made more of an impact wherever they went.

When we returned to the flat in the afternoon the noise of a banging drum drove us up to the roof to investigate. An elephant with an ornate gilt head-dress and feathers was being paraded through the narrow lanes between the houses. Walking behind the elephant were religious devotees and a cart which bore offerings to the gods. This, we were told by the owner of the house who lived on the ground floor, was part of a three-day festival being held at a nearby Hindu temple.

I didn't feel like celebrating when we were blasted from our sleep by firecrackers early the next morning. The girls took it in their stride since they were normally up by six anyway. We were scheduled that morning to hold a programme in a slum school established by the church we'd been in the day before. When we arrived we found about a hundred tiny children of assorted ages crammed into rows on the floor. Bianca did her best to teach a few songs and Benita de Ruiter, from the Netherlands, told a story. I remembered Benita telling me that when her plane came into Bombay she had felt as if she were landing on a different planet: 'Suddenly God is the only one left who really understands you!' Now I watched the teacher trying to insure that Benita's audience didn't get too rowdy. They responded well, and then came the highlight of the school day: the distribution of lunch packets. The children usually took these home to share with all the members of their families. We had our lunch in the tiny home of a church member. The woman had prepared chicken biryani, a treat for most people, but I had trouble with even mildly spiced dishes. It took some tact to resist our hostess' efforts to heap more on my plate. Between the close quarters and the spicy food I was streaming with perspiration.

Later in the afternoon, Veronika Schneeberger and I walked to the market. I was hoping to find tissues for the cold I'd caught before my precious supply of toilet paper ran out. On the way Veronika told me about her life as a pediatric nurse back home in Switzerland. She had always been interested in mission, and these six months with Love India had given her the confidence to apply for longer term service in the subcontinent. Soon, she confided, she would transfer for a few months of medical work among refugees in Pakistan, and then perhaps accept a post as a nurse in an Indian boarding school. 'Now for me there is no turning back!'

On the way back to the flat after making our purchases we ran into another procession. This time there were three massive elephants blocking the road. We paused to watch as priests performed a *puja* (an act of worship), placing offerings and incense in front of the beasts. The elephants were then allowed to crush the coconut shells with their feet and drink the juice. That night we watched the fireworks that signalled the end of the three-day celebration.

Following devotions the next morning, the team divided into twos and threes for house visits. I joined Beena and Bianca and we called upon a mother and her college student daughter who announced right at the start that they were Brahmins. Since this is the highest (priestly) caste for Hindus, we didn't expect to be asked to remain. It turned out that they were both very happy to talk, however, and we spent several hours in remarkable conversation. Bianca and I shared our testimonies and asked questions about Hinduism. The lady of the house showed us the room reserved for family worship, crowded with all manner of statues and pictures of various gods, with dishes of food placed before them as offerings. Although a likeness of Jesus was missing, I knew that Hindus often included him as one of the gods. The lady of the house told us that her husband was an oceanographer. The place certainly suggested a wealthy income. She brought out a lovely silk Punjabi suit from Delhi for our admiration, and even insisted on preparing and serving us a second breakfast. We finally left with a cordial invitation to return soon with other girls on the team.

I wanted to take photos of the girls on the team, and since this was my last afternoon they obligingly arranged themselves in their best saris. After the photo session we took a bus to the park. Sunsets in India are well worth watching and we sat relaxing on the sea wall as the glowing disc of sun sank slowly to the horizon, then disappeared in a last blaze of glory. For a finale we treated ourselves to ice cream in a restaurant. The lights went out soon after our arrival but no one seemed perturbed. The manager produced a candle, we went on eating, and it was business as usual in India!

Sleep eluded me for a long time that night. A mosquito was trapped in my net and it was determined to draw as much blood as it could. I finally eliminated my attacker but the night was so warm, and the mat so hard, that I lay trapped in a feverish half-dream disturbed by visions of garishly coloured gods and goddesses. I woke the next morning unrefreshed, my head aching and the cold decidedly worse. After a cup of *chai* (Indian tea) I hugged my new friends goodbye and took an auto-rickshaw back to the airport.

Hyderabad, the target for the rest of my time in India, was the home of OM's India Centre for Every People. The mission centre was only a few years old and the culmination of a dream: eleven acres within a large compound housing dormitories and guest accommodation, an auditorium to seat 450, classrooms, library, dining-room, offices and an OM Bookshop and warehouse. Besides serving as the mission's training base it was constantly in use by other Christian groups for conferences, which helped to pay expenses.

Hyderabad was a merciful few degrees cooler than Cochin, and although the compound suffered frequent power cuts, especially at prime times in the morning and evening, there was plenty of water. A visitor could even have a hot bath if they first heated the water in a tank, ran it into a bucket and then carried it into the bathroom for a bucket bath. Alternatively one could wait until mid-afternoon. By this time the water in the cold pipes had heated up enough in the sun to provide a warm shower! The drinking water steriliser in the guest kitchen was great entertainment. When the water was ready the steriliser erupted with a series of jolly Christmas tunes. By the time it ran through 'Jingle Bells', 'Santa Claus is Coming to Town' and 'We Wish You a Merry Christmas' I was in holiday mood and ready to deck the halls.

Food at the guest table generally included both Indian and Western fare, but looks could be deceiving. A mouthful of very ordinary-looking vegetables could set you on fire, and no amount of water could quench the flames. Fortunately there was plenty of fruit to fall back on. I had left my tiny jar of emergency peanut butter back in Cochin because one of the girls there had happened to mention a craving for it. I thought her need was greater than mine.

My assignment in Hyderabad was to track down as many exciting reports, stories, and biographical profiles as I possibly could in the limited time I had. Good stories abounded. Most of the leaders had come for meetings that week, and a potential leaders training course was also starting, which had drawn dozens of young people from widely scattered teams. Although OM India had begun about thirty years before with mixed nationalities, visa regulations now severely limited the number of foreign workers. The team of over six hundred men and women was now led entirely by nationals. I marvelled at the quality and commitment of the leadership, the deep respect they showed one another. This and a sense of humour, never far below the surface, defused even the most serious policy or strategy discussions.

It was a special joy to see an old friend I had met five years before in Gorakhpur. At that time Rani had already made the extremely courageous decision never to marry a man who required a dowry. The dowry system was abolished in law years ago, yet in many places it was still in operation. Millions of families who wanted to secure husbands for their daughters struggled with staggering debts. A dowry payment might amount to fifteen times a man's annual wage! Rani had told me of girls who had committed suicide in order to spare their parents the hardship. Other children as young as eight or nine were 'married to the gods' – a euphemism for being sold as temple prostitutes. When the priests cast them off they lived in camps with other such women. Unable to marry since they were already considered married, most supported themselves and their children any way they could. Even the girls who managed to secure husbands were at risk. Dissatisfied parents-in-law might decide to demand additional payment, beating a bride or turning her out unless her family came up with further compensation. Every year some girls were killed. Rani had once been a passenger on a bus when she witnessed a man and older woman in the act of pushing a girl out of a house. 'The girl was on fire', she told me. 'They just stood there, watching her burn to death . . . The driver of the bus warned us not to get involved.'

The growth of infanticide in India could also be linked in part to the dowry system. Poor families regarded the birth of a daughter as an economic disaster. Enterprising doctors were now taking ultrasound equipment from village to village so that women could determine the sex of their unborn infants. Female foetuses were then usually aborted. Many women would continue the cycle of conception and abortion until they produced a son. Those who couldn't afford ultrasound simply waited until after birth to do away with unwanted little girls through suffocation, poison or abandonment. Mothers who resisted this course of action ran the risk of being thrown out themselves.

When Rani refused to conform to the dowry system, her father severed links with her for four years. Her grandmother died refusing to speak to her. But although everyone was quite certain that Rani had doomed herself to being single for good, God had honoured her stand. At thirty-four, he gave her a Christian partner willing to accept her for herself alone. Now at the Centre I saw Rani as a married woman, happily anticipating the birth of her first child. She and her husband were working for OM in her home state of Tamil Nadu. The caste system was still very strong in this area, she admitted, even among believers. Some churches were made up entirely of members of a certain caste, and non-members were not welcome. Rani described several cases where girls who had attempted to marry outside their caste were ostracised or even killed.

During the first part of my stay in Hyderabad I shared a room with Mrs Juliet Thomas. Juliet was the founder and director of the first women's prayer network in India and on my interview list, so the arrangement couldn't have suited me better. Juliet was quite a woman. She had grown up in Malaysia and met her Indian husband on the day she married him. For the next twenty-two years she was his devoted wife as well as a mother, teacher in a mission school, and the Evangelical Fellowship of India's first Secretary for

Women's Ministries. It was in 1991 that she implemented her vision to unite and mobilise Christian women through a nationwide prayer network. 'Women in India face two obstacles,' Juliet writes in her book, *After God's Own Heart*. 'The church's attitude towards them, and their attitude toward themselves. We've been told for so long that we're non-persons that we do not seriously believe that God can work through us! Women need to hear again, in loud and clear tones, that they can reach their full potential in Christ. Then there is no limit to what they can do!' Juliet explained that the objective of the Arpana Network was to teach women how to pray effectively. Prayer seminars held in key cities encouraged the formation of 'prayer triplets', groups of three committed to regular intercession for specific targets. 'I have no idea how many women are involved now. We've gone to places we've never been before and found women meeting in triplets. I could never have imagined the way the Lord is putting the whole thing together. And we are seeing reconciliation and changed lives.'

The Divakarans were another highly motivated couple. Diva, as he liked to be called, had grown up as a Hindu and practised his religion faithfully through his teens. Once he had walked forty-five miles to reach a certain temple, where he had then sat and fasted for fifteen days. But the young man became more and more unhappy with his circumstances. Eventually he began to have thoughts of suicide. At the age of nineteen he travelled to New Delhi and bought two bottles of poison. Just afterwards he ran into an OM team on the streets. The men persuaded him to buy a Bible, along with a book entitled *Life After Death*. But Divakaran wasn't interested in reading. With a last desperate prayer that if Jesus was really God, he would somehow intervene to save him, Diva went to an isolated place outside the city and drank the poison. Villagers found him soon after and police rushed Diva to a hospital. By chance, they came across the address of OM in the Bible he carried. The authorities contacted the OM office and one of the men on the team went to see Diva. Finding him still unconscious, he left behind a copy of Billy Graham's *Peace With God*.

When Divakaran recovered he was certain that Jesus Christ had intervened in answer to his prayer. Diva surrendered his heart and life to him, and for the first time he felt the inner happiness he had always longed for. Diva planned to stay with his new friends for a week after his discharge and then return home. But the week turned into a lifetime with OM. In subsequent years he had seen several other members of his family also put their trust in Jesus Christ. Divakaran was now serving as Associate Executive Director of OM India.

As I talked to the young people who had come for leadership training I discovered that a fair number of them had come from Hindu or Muslim backgrounds. One girl was originally named in honour of a goddess and brought up in a high caste Brahmin family. It was while she was taking a nurse's training course that she went with friends to see a film called *Jesus*. It changed her life.

'I went home and threw out all the photos I had of the gods. When my mother found me I told her, "These aren't gods. God is in my heart!" And when the rest of the family came to beat me I said, "You can beat me and you can kill me, but I won't change. I won't give up Jesus Christ." They couldn't understand. I was a very proud person, but I went to Sunday School with the small children because I wanted to learn. And God filled the empty space in my heart.'

It was impossible to listen to such stories without feeling

humbled. Here were young men and women who had paid a high price for following Jesus, and never looked back. Shankar was another such person. I had known him for several years, but on this trip he told me he was leaving his job as leader of the work in Andhra Pradesh to work among his own people.

'My family has always been very much devoted to the gods and goddesses,' he explained. 'We are members of the Lingayat people in Karnataka. The Lingayats are an offshoot of Brahminism. My grandfather was a well-known fortune-teller and my uncle was a poet of verses to the gods. But when I started attending a Christian school I began reading the Bible. Psalm 115 shocked me.

> Why do the nations say, 'Where is their God?' Our God is in heaven; he does whatever pleases him. But their idols are silver and gold, made by the hands of men. They have mouths, but cannot speak, eyes, but they cannot see; they have ears, but cannot hear, noses, but they cannot smell . . . Those who make them will be like them, and so will all who trust in them (Ps 115: 2–6, 8).

'I'd never thought of idols in that way. I searched the Vedas and went to the temples, but I didn't find any answers. Again I read about Jesus in the Bible, and went to a Christian meeting. At the end of it, with fear and trembling, I stood up and gave myself to the Lord. I was so filled with joy and peace from that moment! I kept my new faith quiet from my family for a year, but you can't hide the truth. When my family saw me read the Bible they were upset. They tore it from me and kicked me. They believed Jesus is a god, all right, but the problem was saying Jesus is *the* God.

Eventually I had to leave home. My father told everyone if I ever came home he'd break my legs and shut me up in a room. I joined OM so that I could grow and develop. But now I want to go back and work with the Lingayat people.' When I asked if he was afraid, Shankar looked me straight in the eyes. He admitted his fear frankly. 'I know it will be very hard. I will go alone first, and build friendships. Hopefully later we can have a team. But my whole desire is to see some of my people come to the Lord.'

On my last day I arranged to interview members of the Good Shepherd team. These people were responsible for setting up schools, literacy classes and medical work in the slums of Hyderabad, Bombay, Calcutta and, most recently, Bhopal. Lissy Joseph, who led the team in Hyderabad, confided that it was easy to become emotionally and physically drained.

She cited the case of a family they met who, like so many others, had moved to the city hoping for a new start. The father's bicycle repair work did not make nearly enough money to support the family. Life in the slums went from bad to worse when he started drinking. Husband and wife fought bitterly. On top of everything else the woman suffered from seizures and their eldest son had leprosy. When the Good Shepherd team visited them they were at rock bottom: no food, no clothes. Desperate. The team went every day and took the children to school and helped clothe them. They provided some medical help. Now the family's situation had turned around. The mother was healed and all but the father – who is afraid to leave his Hindu idols – were attending worship services. They were strong in their faith. 'How much can we help each person and for how long? are questions we are always asking,' sighed Lissy. Caring for India's destitute was sometimes dangerous, often frustrating, and always overwhelming. But it reminded me of the story of the old man who went walking along the beach early one morning. He began to notice a young man ahead of him who was picking up starfish and throwing them into the sea. Catching up with the young man, the older man asked what he was doing. The boy replied that the starfish would die if they were left out of the water any longer. The old man couldn't understand. 'The beach goes on for miles,' he said. 'How can your effort make any difference?' The young man looked at the starfish in his hand, then threw it into the life-giving sea. 'It makes a difference to this one,' he said.

It was time to return to Bombay for my flight back to London. The auto-rickshaw ride to the airport was harrowing. The twin cities of Hyderabad and Secunderabad had a population of over five million, and going anywhere was enough to send anyone's blood pressure over the top, especially if you were aware that a good many drivers on the road never bothered with obtaining a driver's licence, and those who did could purchase one through the mail without a test! To add to the adventure of travel, many roads were paved with a width of only one and a half lanes on each side. This was just wide enough to encourage overtaking buses and trucks to scrape by. I suppressed screams as a number of times we narrowly missed being crushed like a tin can. The driver seemed undaunted to it all, absorbed in telling me about his wife and the coming birth of their first child.

During the flight between Hyderabad and Bombay I found myself staring through the window at the vast expanse of land below. In spite of India's vast population – numbering almost as many people as Africa and South America combined – there were surprisingly large tracts of uninhabited and probably uninhabitable land, scorched and unfriendly-looking. As we neared Bombay I could clearly pick out the numerous slum patches with their miles of corrugated tin roofs sandwiched between the taller, more affluent-looking buildings.

To my relief Raju, an elderly Indian worker, stood faithfully at the terminal exit with a sign bearing my name. I had an early morning flight to London so he settled me into a nearby hotel favoured by impoverished missionaries. I felt safe enough when the door was bolted, and although the linen was stained I was sure it was clean enough. I had a bottle of water, some crackers and the indispensable toilet paper. After killing off all the mosquitoes I could find, I lay down for a few hours' sleep. In spite of my precautions I awoke with two rings of mosquito bites decorating my ankles and a steady whining in my ears. I rose at 4 a.m and was ready to leave by five. Airport security was tight – a seemingly endless round of baggage checks and x-rays plus two body searches. Perhaps this had something to do with the flight being routed through Kuwait. Once more I found myself in the smoking section, but since the inflight movie was a repeat of *The Client* I got to see how it ended! Four hours later we were in Kuwait, a flat, barren landscape coloured only by the jetting orange-red flames of oil wells. A change of planes and then we were off again for the second leg of six hours. But this time I was in non-smoking! However, hopes of curling up in the extra seats beside me were dashed when two Kuwaiti men in robes and head-dresses took them. I sat reading my New Testament, probably horrifying the men by their proximity to an infidel.

I was just hungrily anticipating a snack when a boy two rows ahead suddenly vomitted all over the aisle.

The attendants had vanished into thin air as attendants sometimes do, and no one moved to clean up the mess for at least twenty minutes. By that time my appetite had definitely dwindled. It was also obvious by then that the boy had something more than an upset stomach. He had begun thrashing about and screaming and his mother was wringing her hands in anguish. Suddenly all the attendants converged *en masse*. A doctor was paged, and passengers clogged the aisle to try to get a good view of what was going on. The poor child kept crying out at intervals and was finally carried to a space further back where he could lie on the floor. The doctors consulted, and airline personnel scuttled away for various items. Everyone in the cabin was in a state of suspense. Finally the boy was apparently given something to make him fall asleep. It was, we learned later, a case of diabetic shock. I saw the boy later and he appeared much improved.

We were spared any further drama during the flight. The person dispatched to meet me at Heathrow had remembered to bring a coat. England was still in the throes of winter. I fingered the thin material of my Punjabi suit and thought how easy it was to cross the geographical boundaries of our modern world. It was a far more daring thing to venture into unknown realms of the spirit. The Indian men and women I had met had managed to do so. In the presence of other gods, they were daily offering themselves as a living sacrifice for the one true God. And I felt honoured to know them.

14

Far East assignment

Moving slowly through a rare snow shower in early March 1995, it was hard to believe that in another thirteen hours I would be exchanging the traffic jams of London for Hong Kong. The Pearl of the Orient was the starting-line of a seven-week news-gathering marathon that would take me to six different countries in the Far East. The commitment to cover a Love Philippines outreach during Easter week had somewhat expanded. I wanted to make the most of my ticket. If only more people knew what God was doing in these out-of-the-way places, I reasoned, perhaps they would get involved. Royalties from my first book about OM, *Footsteps in the Sea*, arrived just in time to meet some of the expenses.

Tim Wright couldn't be released from other responsi-bilities to accompany me, but he offered to sort out the details of my itinerary. I was excited about this trip. I was also a bit jittery, knowing that most of the time I would be exploring unfamiliar territory. I was, however, travelling with a companion who knew every inch.

I had been introduced to Hong Kong five years before, and remembered well the spectacular, if nerve-rattling, touchdown in Kai Tak Airport. If you land in daylight and your eyes are still open, you can see the South China Sea lapping both sides of the runway. After that you probably won't look down or around so much as up – the skyline of Hong Kong Central is surely one of the wonders of the modern world.

OM leader Stella Chan was an old friend, who generously gave me the use not only of her flat, but also of half her bed. Space is one of the most precious commodities in Hong Kong. Flats tend to be small, and Stella already had a niece living with her who was also working for OM. Each day that Stella, Violet and I set out together for the mission's office in Kowloon we caught a tram, and then transferred either to the Star Ferry or the MTR (Mass Transit Railway). My preference was always the ferry. Although it was crowded and a slower way to go, the crossing offered a panoramic view of the harbour by night or day.

Hong Kong's countdown was obviously on. Everyone in the territory might be going about their daily business as usual, but they also had their eyes firmly fixed on 1997. Hong Kong's giant neighbour was already shuffling its feet on the doorstep, eager to repossess this economic jewel. Changes were inevitable. But Stella Chan was one person who looked forward to even greater opportunities in the future. 'When China opens, the believers will come. And it's time for people from mainland China to share with the rest of the world. If there comes a time when we can't send people from Hong Kong to other places, then we'll work in Hong Kong. We'll do whatever the Lord allows us to do without fear. And with the confidence that God has a plan for OM Hong Kong to exist.'

Meanwhile, Stella and her team intended to make full use of the 800 days that were left. Hong Kong's thousand plus churches needed to form closer ties. They needed to be encouraged to send more people into missions abroad, and do something about the needs right on their doorstep. Already, a hundred men, women and children were leaving the People's Republic every day to make their home in what they saw as the land of opportunity. These were the legal immigrants, supposedly joining relatives. Everyone knew thousands of other mainlanders slipped over the border illegally.

Most newcomers were instantly identifiable. Their clothes and their behaviour lacked the sophistication of Hong Kong residents. Mainlanders also spoke a different language, Mandarin rather than Cantonese or English. The majority were unable to afford the high cost of living in Hong Kong so they settled in the squatter areas.

The daily trickle of immigrants would soon increase to a flood, yet neither the Hong Kong government nor the Church seemed prepared to deal with it. That's what had prompted OM to initiate a new ministry called Heart to Heart. The aim is to reach out – and get local churches to reach out – to the immigrants. The first targets are those who are already Christians, helping them with their problems, getting them into fellowship with other believers. They are the best ones to reach their own people! But the team also aim to show other new arrivals that God cares about them. They can assess their needs and link them with available government help. They are already producing testimony and Gospel tracts in simple Mandarin for churches to distribute.

Violet Hau was in charge of getting the new Heart to Heart project up and running. She explained that many believers wanted to do something, but they didn't know what. OM meant to co-ordinate the resources that existed, keep the churches informed, and encourage individuals to be personally involved. A special team would also be recruited to work directly with immigrants.

Most visitors come prepared to spend a lot of money in Hong Kong. For those who'd rather invest their time in exploration, there is plenty to reward them. I had scouted around a lot of the territory on my last trip while visiting Love Hong Kong teams. On a free day this time I was happy to accept a friend's invitation to see something of the 'other' Hong Kong – a few of the 235 islands not usually visited by tourists. Joanne Soh, co-ordinator for OM's annual Love Asia summer campaign, was my guide. We took a train north to the Chinese University, bought a picnic lunch, and caught the mailboat out of Tolo Harbour. The weather was miserable, and the first island we passed was depressing – a detention centre for Vietnamese refugees. Many of the islands we saw were mountainous and sparsely populated. But when we disembarked and walked around a tiny fishing community called Tap Mun Chau (Grass Island), I was in my element. Here was the Chinese version of a Maine island. It even smelled the same! But there were sampans in the harbour instead of dories and lobster boats. And instead of a friendly old salt on the dock we ran into a no-nonsense police officer who checked our credentials carefully, ever alert for smugglers.

Knowing that I was anxious to meet recent immigrants, Violet took me to a squatters' church in Tseun Wan on Sunday. The church had been pioneered by Bill Wong, Executive Director of the Hong Kong Squatter Fellowship. I had half-expected the meeting to be held in a shack, but it was in an ordinary flat, and Bill spoke simply from Psalm 139 on how to pray. I enjoyed the lively singing, the warmth and friendliness of the people. One badly scarred woman gave a moving testimony of how God had preserved her life in a fire that destroyed her dwelling. Such tragedies were all too common among the squatters, I was told, but the people could expect little help from the authorities.

Violet and I were happy to stay for the customary fellowship meal after the service. The elderly believer who sat beside me concentrated on putting food in my bowl when it escaped the inexpert grasp of my chopsticks. He spoke English, so I asked what he thought about the coming takeover by China. 'The best way to get ready for 1997 is to strengthen ourselves inside, spiritually,' he said. 'And to live as simply as possible.' It sounded like good advice.

Violet had hoped to persuade someone to show us through some of the squatter areas, but no one was available and it was obviously unwise to wander on our own. We decided to ignore the blustery weather and take the tram up to Victoria Peak instead. The panorama of the city and harbour from fifteen hundred feet above sea level was not a sight one could tire of – even when being blown inside out. When hunger finally overtook us we returned to Kowloon for a hamburger and fries in the least expensive McDonald's in the world. You may wonder how I could possibly have chosen to eat something so mundane when surrounded by all the marvellous food of the Orient? Let me assure you that I love Cantonese cuisine. But rice or noodles three times a day does wear a bit thin when you're not used to it. I admit that I too used to censure those tourists who always make a beeline for the nearest fast-food chains. Now I'm a bit more understanding. In a new and strange environment, a person's senses can reach overload. When that happens you find yourself groping for something that's safe and familiar, that resembles home. Even if it's only McDonald's golden arches!

Violet suggested that we attend St Andrew's that evening. The Anglican church had evangelistic services in English, and judging by the size of the crowd it was popular with Chinese students as well as other nationalities. During the service a young British professional shared the riveting story of how God had given him and his wife a new start in life after atheism and a near divorce. The previous year when their situation had reached crisis-point the couple had decided to visit a church pastored by Jackie Pullinger, author of *Chasing the Dragon*. The message they heard led them both to put their faith in Jesus Christ.

On my last morning in Hong Kong I faced a cold wind to take a long walk. I wanted once more to absorb the bustle of the streets: the sights and smells and sounds so very unique to the Far East. How could I ever describe the open-air food markets spilling over with every conceivable kind of fresh and dried fish, sharkfins, even desiccated snakes? Apothecary shops with their neat rows of labelled jars offered medicines never found – or even imagined – in the West. Religious stalls were stuffed with colourful banners, incense, paper money and statues of gods. Even ordinary food stores held extraordinary items like bottled snake bile. The walk sharpened my appetite for a delicious *dim sum* lunch with Stella's family before I boarded the plane for Singapore.

High-tech, high-rise Singapore was a lot different from what I had imagined. For one thing it was a lot hotter. The island's proximity to the equator assures a steamy year-round temperature and Singaporeans have learned to dress for the tropics in light, practical materials. I surrendered all attempts at looking chic and shifted into survival mode: T-shirts, shorts and sleeveless shifts. I dragged my hair back from my face and even gave up on make-up after it melted: the ultimate humiliation.

My hosts were a delightful young Chinese couple who had only been married a year. Their spacious flat was in a new housing block located very near the end of one of the train lines. Once equipped with a map and a value ticket (good for either buses and trains), I found getting around on my own surprisingly simple. Singapore's efficient public transport system is, in fact, the major explanation for its uncrowded roads. That and the prohibitive cost of buying a car. Owners of vehicles over ten years old are further discouraged by having to pay additional taxes! Singaporeans themselves joke that their little country is a 'fine' place. Watch out or you'll be fined for littering, for eating on the train, and for smoking or spitting in the wrong place. You can even be fined 150 Singapore dollars for not flushing a public toilet, although I'm not sure how they enforce that one. If you're not fined, you can be caned. If you forget to pack chewing-gum, you won't find anyone in Singapore who will sell it to you: it's against the law. As for gun possession, that carries the death penalty. But all the rules and regulations have had their effect. You will seldom find a cleaner environment, or a society that has succeeded better in keeping a lid on violence. Residents are so compliant with government programmes that a 'Stop At Two' campaign to control the population, launched a few years ago, proved too effective. The birth rate fell to an alarming average 1.4 children per couple, causing leaders to rethink their strategy.

As I rode the trains and buses around the island I gazed out at a never-ending vista of concrete. The jungles that had originally suggested the name 'Singapura' – Lion City – are, alas, no more. Only a generation or two ago, individual landholdings or *kampongs* boasted their own gardens and yards for chickens. These too have almost all been replaced by housing blocks and shopping centres. Elderly *kampong*-owners have been forced into apartments. The fact is the 620 square kilometres of this republic have become far too precious to allow the luxury of single dwellings – except for a handful of the very rich. To glimpse the country's abundant flora and fauna these days, the visitor must resort to the Botanical Gardens and Zoo.

Signs for the MRT (Mass Rapid Transit system) were posted in the republic's four major languages: English, Chinese, Malay and Tamil. Around me sat shirt-and-tie businessmen, sari and sarong clad women, and teenagers in shorts and T-shirts. But Singapore had learned how to handle its mixed population. The peoples' commitment to multi-ethnic harmony was reflected in their Pledge of Allegiance: 'We, the citizens of Singapore, pledge ourselves as one united people regardless of race, language or religion to build a democratic society based on justice and equality, so as to achieve happiness, prosperity and progress for our nation.' 'Prosperity' and 'progress' were key words in this culture. Singapore had succeeded in becoming the number one in global business communication, and its citizens were the most computer literate in the world. The republic also boasted the busiest international port and one of the finest airports. Even school age children felt the pressure to become the best and the brightest. Most took extra-curricular lessons or tutoring to enhance their future chances.

Buddhism, Taoism, Islam, Hinduism and Christianity all added their colour to the social tapestry. Chinese religions claimed over half of the population. About 15 per cent followed Islam, 14 per cent Christianity. But churches were multiplying and becoming more affluent, ranging in size from forty to over four thousand.

With approximately 60 per cent of the world's population living within a 1000-mile radius of Singapore, the island was a natural springboard for mission outreach. Small wonder that OM's East Asia area leader, Rodney Hui, made it his base too. I was impressed to learn that local churches gave 50 per cent or more of their budget to missions. One of OM's goals was to arrange hands-on experience for the growing number of church groups that wanted to give more than money. 'This year we're arranging mission trips to Turkey, Central Asia, Pakistan and India, the Philippines, and Mongolia,' field leader Kenneth Bong told me. 'One leading church plans to send every one of its 120 cell groups on a mission trip next year, and we're one of the principal agencies they're approaching for help.'

OM regularly arranged weekend outreaches for church groups in nearby Malaysia as well. Singaporean believers, maintained Kenneth, had had enough teaching to be ready to be exposed to real situations. One of the most immediate problems facing Kenneth and his staff was the relocation of the mission office. They had been forced to move nine times in the past because of rising rents. Now that the present landlord was planning to repossess his property, OM leaders had decided it was time to purchase rather than rent. I spent an afternoon office-hunting with Rodney and Kenneth, looking at several properties an agent had lined up for their inspection. As in Hong Kong, space was scarce – and expensive. Our expedition wasn't successful and it would be another five months before they found what they were looking for.

When the office closed for a holiday Rodney asked me along on a family outing to Sentosa Island, Singapore's answer to Disneyland. While the Hui family swam in the aqua park I took advantage of the free monorail and bus system to visit the Asian Village, Coralarium, Maritime Museum, and nature trails. I ended up on a palm-fringed beach that would measure up to anyone's dream of a tropical island paradise. I only wish it could have lasted longer. But Singapore had treasure enough even without Sentosa. Orchids and flowers of every colour delighted the eye wherever one looked. One evening I joined the staff after work at the open-air Satay Club to enjoy a Malaysian speciality – chunks of chicken and pork skewered, barbecued and dipped in a spicy sauce. Afterwards we took a stroll around the gaslit waterfront of Clarke Quay. Lined with elegant restaurants and shops, this formerly notorious port area was now *the* fashionable nightspot for the young and upwardly mobile.

Part of the fascination of Singapore is its ambience. In spite of its contemporary face, the glass and concrete image it presents to the Western world, interesting wrinkles of the past are never far below. Tourists may choose to insulate themselves in sophisticated Orchard Street malls or travel to the totally different worlds of Chinatown and Little India. Yet another slice of history is to be found in Singapore's most famous hotel, Raffles. Modernised from its more humble beginnings in the last century, the place retains the polished wood and potted plant décor of colonial days, along with a definite, rather smugly superior, atmosphere. For me some of that aura came from knowing that writers like Somerset Maugham and Noel Coward had been guests there. For others the attradtion is undoubtedly the infamous Singapore Sling, first created at Raffles' Long Bar.

Singapore teased my imagination and I knew I was leaving with much still unexplored. But it was time to move on from one of the smallest nations to one of the largest, Indonesia.

15

God's emeralds

Jakarta definitely falls into the 'off the beaten track' category for most people. Even those who have heard of Java are a little vague about its location. Small wonder, since it's just one out of thirteen and a half thousand islands that make up the Republic of Indonesia. Mrs Suharto calls this archipelago straddling the Pacific and Indian Oceans a 'string of emeralds on the Equator'. But if you dream of unspoiled island paradises, don't go to Jakarta. Jakarta is Indonesia's capital and the hub of all political, religious and social activity. It is also grossly overcrowded and polluted, its population of nine million expected to triple by the year 2000.

Indonesia's government officially tolerates all religions, but Islam obviously takes a starring role. President Suharto appointed five members of a powerful Islamic group to his cabinet in 1993 and others were granted similarly high positions. Criticism of the government does not go down well, however. Publications that do not toe the official line have found themselves banned, their journalists behind bars. In 1965, an attempted Communist takeover prompted the government to rule that every citizen had to carry an identification card which stated the bearer's religion. This law has generated some misleading statistics. Although I.D. cards indicate 82 per cent of Indonesians are Muslims, a large number are in practice more dedicated to animism and ancestor worship.

Islamists call their programme to take over Indonesia the 'Green Revolution'. Sometimes their efforts are subtle, like replacing the blue street signs with green ones; sometimes they are more obvious – as in their declared intention of building a mosque in every village. One common conversion strategy is the promotion of marriages between Muslim men and non-Muslim women. Another is transmigration, the transplanting of people from overcrowded cities like Jakarta to less populated areas with the help of government funds. As a result of this the island of Ambon, once 100 per cent Christian, is now 55 per cent Muslim.

Freedom of religion notwithstanding, many schools compel children to repeat Islamic prayers every day. Teachers may also make free with false or misleading statements about Christianity or the person of Jesus Christ. Christian parents told me their children sometimes returned home in tears after being subjected to their Muslim classmates' taunts. Christian adults face job discrimination. A promotion may be withheld unless an employee consents to becoming a Muslim. All they are required to do is repeat the *shahada*, the Islamic statement of faith: 'There is no God but Allah and Mohammad is his Prophet.' In self-defence, loyal Christians have started their own businesses or work for foreign firms.

Churches must get a permit before carrying out renovations or they can be – and are – closed down. Nor will the government grant permission for building new churches. The leaders of one Chinese church that I saw under construction said they overcame this obstacle by registering the building as an auditorium or meeting centre.

'At this time in Indonesia it's very hard to share the gospel,' observed Meli, an OM worker. 'If we do, we are accused of forcing our religion on other people. Jehovah's Witnesses went door-to-door and gave out tracts some years ago and after that it wasn't allowed. We can only give literature to people quietly and individually.' Still, outreach was possible if it was conducted with sensitivity. OM's leader, Bagus, described how seven churches had been burned in East Java the previous year, after an outsider to the area preached and gave out tracts. 'But when we went to Sumatra last year and showed the film *Jesus*, sixty Muslims came to the Lord. They were baptised and they remain faithful today. The difference is that I used to live there. I know the people and the situation, and we did it in the acceptable way.'

Bagus had sailed with me on the *Logos* around South America, just before the ship ran aground. I recalled that I was impressed even then by his linguistic and musical skills, the warmth and enthusiasm of his faith. The fact that he was raised in Indonesia by a Muslim woman after his own home broke up made his testimony all the more remarkable. After the shipwreck of the *Logos* Bagus had served on the *Doulos*, and when the *Logos II* was launched, he had transferred once again at the request of leaders. It was on this ship that he and a girl he had known back in Indonesia, Delores, fell in love. When they decided to marry the mission asked them to consider taking over leadership of OM Indonesia.

The couple were reluctant to leave the ship ministry. Bagus knew that he could never enjoy the same freedom and fruitfulness in his own country. But they understood the need, and Bagus went to study for a theology degree in

Singapore. The pair took up the reins of mission leadership two years ago. Now inadequate finances and staff, sickness, the lack of vision in local churches, and most of all a sense of isolation had brought them to the point of giving up.

We had plenty of time to talk during our ten days together. Bagus had set up a number of speaking engagements for me, and travelling to each one meant spending many hours sitting in traffic jams. Delores told me that before getting their own vehicle they had used a bicycle and local buses to get around Jakarta. The long hours of exposure to the intense heat and air pollution had eroded Bagus's health. I wasn't surprised. I felt wrung out after just a single return trip. But although the speaking appointments weren't something I had planned, each contact with Bible students and church members helped to enlighten me about the situation in Indonesia.

A few hours in the amazing new Purna Bhakti Pertiwi Museum gave me some more insights. The museum was designed to show the treasures of china, precious stones and works of art presented over the years to President and Mrs Sujarto by visiting VIPs. Bagus, Connie, Meli and I spent most of another day sight-seeing in 'Beautiful Mini-Indonesia,' a mammoth theme park that re-creates Indonesia's varied island cultures.

One Saturday we left behind the city's pollution and headed for the clean air of the mountains. The mountainsides were thickly planted, for this was tea plantation country. Bagus stopped to let me take photos of the Sundanese women picking the tea leaves. The women were very dark, in spite of the broad bamboo hats they wore to shield themselves from the sun. Their long hours of back-breaking work earned them about fifty cents a day, Bagus told me. The Sundanese were one of the largest unreached people groups in the world. They were Muslims, officially, but their personal faith was strongly influenced by animism. Before leaving the plantation I picked some leaves to press in my Bible. I didn't want to forget these people.

Bagus and Delores's hospitality touched me deeply. Their small home was already over-crowded with two baby daughters, Bagus's sister who was attending the university, plus two live-in helpers (one a Muslim girl they had taken in out of kindness after she became pregnant and was thrown out by her family). But somehow they had managed to provide me with privacy for sleeping and writing. The toilet was Western style, which was flushed manually with pails of water, and the cold bucket baths provided refreshment from the equatorial heat.

My friends had even arranged for me to spend a day and night in the luxurious home of board members. The T—'s were highly regarded professionals and their house was large and beautifully furnished. The guest suite I occupied contained a queen-size bed and a private, tiled bathroom with hot water. There was even a cook to provide me with exquisite meals! I spent the day writing, catching up on BBC news via cable TV, and interviewing OM Indonesia's pioneer leader Meggy Pelupessy. But as much as I appreciated the oasis, I was happy to return to the home of Bagus and Dolores. My goal in coming to Indonesia was to come alongside these workers, to understand their burdens and their vision so that I could communicate them to the rest of the world.

I contracted a stomach bug during my last few days, and when I got to the airport for my midnight flight to Korea I must have been more tired than I thought. I checked in at the wrong gate and just missed taking off for Japan! As it turned out my flight was delayed anyway, until 2.30 a.m.

When I left the plane in Seoul six and a half hours later I was nearly blown off my feet. A temperature drop of fifteen degrees and gale force winds gave me an idea of how it felt to be freeze-dried. A row of Koreans waited at the customs exit with placards, but unfortunately there were none with my name on. My heart sank. I placed myself in a conspicuous place, but when everyone else on my plane finally drifted away I had to face facts. No one was going to claim me. I quashed the impulse to panic, exchanged some money for a telephone card and began dialling. None of my colleagues were home, of course; it was Sunday morning. I tried again and then resigned myself to a long wait. My Indonesian bug was still tap-dancing on my stomach, making it necessary to pay frequent trips to the toilet. I longed for a corner to curl up and sleep. At long last, around mid-afternoon, my calls succeeded in reaching Korean field leader Joseph Lee. 'I didn't know you were coming!' he exclaimed, sending my hopes into a nosedive. I don't know which of us was more dismayed. Tim had assured me he had faxed confirmations to all the country leaders before I left. Everything had gone smoothly up to this point, but I guess I should have expected at least one hitch.

Since Joseph clearly didn't know what to do with me on this Sunday afternoon already crowded with obligations, I volunteered to find a hotel for the night. I had, fortunately, been furnished with an American Express card for just such an emergency. Joseph was relieved. He gave me instructions for taking the bus into the city centre where he met me and drove me to reasonably priced accommodation near the OM office. When I became better acquainted with the exquisite courtesy that is so much a part of Korean culture, I understood Joseph's dilemma. Relatives were already sharing his family's apartment at that time so there was absolutely no room to receive another guest. As for the single women on our OM staff, they all lived with their families as unmarried women did in this culture, so they could offer me no accommodation either. Then too there was the bed problem. Koreans slept on mats on the floor, but Joseph wouldn't dream of offering the same arrangement to a Western guest. I assured him later, of course, that it didn't matter. In OM we learned to sleep wherever we were put, or we didn't survive. But I must admit that the comforts of Hotel Sunshine that night were more than welcome. The next morning Joseph escorted me to the OM office. The poor man had probably spent a troubled night over how to handle this journalist. The fact was, the whole OM staff was due to leave immediately for their biannual retreat. I could not remain alone in Seoul, he insisted, a stranger unable to speak the language. The only solution was to take me along.

I was delighted. A retreat sounded like an ideal way to become acquainted with our office staff from Seoul, Pusan, and Daeku. A few days together should give me all the interview time and stories I needed. My delight doubled when I learned where the retreat was to be held: Cheju Island, a favourite holiday getaway off the southern tip of the country. Korean OMers really knew how to do things right. The mission planned to open a recruiting office very soon in Cheju, and one of the churches on the island was loaning the team vehicles and arranging our accommodation.

Cheju is famous for its volcanic rock, its ceaseless winds, and its women-divers. The latter were widows of local fishermen who gathered their living from the floor of the sea. But I will most remember Cheju Island for my new friends – oh, and the food, of course!

The Korean people are said to be quick to laugh, and slow to show anger. Although I was the only outsider among the sixteen staff members on the retreat, they never made me feel I didn't belong. Nor was their acceptance merely polite. I felt warmth and affection from each person, even if it meant they had to stretch their English to the limit. Laughter was useful. I was unused to the Korean practice of addressing strangers by their surnames. When Joseph called me 'Meroff' I must have looked startled, for everyone jumped on him. The use of 'Debbie' became universal. We enjoyed exploring the natural beauty of the island together, and when the team held their business and study sessions I was content to work at my laptop. Joseph asked me to give a devotional message one morning. It was a privilege to share with these brothers and sisters through translation, just as they shared with me.

OM was only six years old in this country, but it had ambitious goals. Some 350 Koreans had already been sent into short-or long-term missionary service and Joseph hoped to increase that number to 100 a year. Candidates were required to have a college degree and undergo comprehensive tests and interviews before they were accepted into a four-month training programme.

I quickly grew to admire the Korean character, and the Korean countryside. But their cuisine was quite another matter. My first lunch with the team featured kimchee (cabbage pickled in garlic, salt and chili peppers) and rice, cold fish, cold tea, an assortment of dishes I couldn't identify, and – the highlight – a bowl of soup which contained three or four molluscs. I was told to extract the inhabitants of the shells with my chopsticks. Easier said than done. After toying with the things unsuccessfully for ten minutes I abandoned all attempts at fastidiousness and tore out the hapless animals with my fingers. Victoriously I plopped it into my mouth. The shock was grotesque. Nor could I find anything else on the table that tasted less than awful. When the bite of fish turned out to be a mouthful of bones I decided this week was as good a time as any to lose weight. The Koreans, however, couldn't get enough of the local seafood. One day I spied a kettle full of fish heads and seaweed being prepared for lunch. Bread from a local shop saved me from potential disaster.

During the week a local believer and his wife treated the whole team to sushi at a Japanese restaurant. I was still getting used to Korean food and wasn't sure I was ready for a further exotic experience, but everyone assured me I'd love it. Raw fish was also very expensive so it wasn't likely I would get another opportunity to try it. They pressed me to try all of the delicacies: starfish eggs, octopus . . . the courses seemed to go on and on. I endeavoured to hide my leftovers under lettuce leaves. My legs were also giving me trouble, unused as I was to sitting with them tucked under me for such a long period. Everyone grinned as I squirmed and ended up half-reclining.

When it came time to leave Cheju Island, the Pusan contingent took me along to their city. Pusan had five million residents and was Korea's second city, a major recruiting centre for OM. Pusan also happened to be the home of the Park family, former shipmates from the *Logos II*. Min Hwan, Hea Sook and their two sons were now serving with Korean Harbour Mission. When Hea Sook learned that I was in the country she called and asked me to stay with them. It was a lovely final weekend. My friend took charge of showing me the city and, when she learned I had left my only good pair of shoes in Singapore, bought new ones for me. She even saw to it that I got my hair trimmed. It *had* grown rather shaggy during the past weeks!

I was tempted to acquire some warm clothes, as well. The winds of the port city cut like a knife and worsened the inevitable cold I'd developed. But at night I was snug. Like all homes in Korea, the floor on which I slept in the Park home was heated at night, a very clever idea indeed.

Sunday was my first opportunity to attend a church service in this country. I was looking forward to it. The amazing growth of Korea's Christian Church during the last decades had become the stuff of legends. In Seoul I had exclaimed at the size of a church that Joseph Lee and I were passing. He laughed, and told me that a small church numbered approximately fifteen hundred members, an average church five to ten thousand, and a large church over over thirty thousand! And believers were truly committed. Daily 5 a.m. prayer meetings were commonplace, and well attended. While I was with the Parks, Min Hwan followed the usual once-a-week practice of spending a night on a prayer mountain.

The morning service at the Presbyterian church I attended was formal. Everyone was very well dressed, and I silently blessed my friend for my new shoes. Although I couldn't understand the language, I found the singing of the choir and congregation most inspiring – all Koreans seemed to have marvellous voices. The congregation remained after the service for a simple communal lunch, and then separated for classes. Min Hwan asked me to take part of the class he taught to young people. At 2 p.m. there was another service, less formal than the first, and then we were finished for the day. I was surprised when three girls from Min Hwan's class came home with us. Hea Sook told me they were quite fascinated to meet an unmarried woman of my advanced years, and couldn't wait to ask all kinds of questions. Of course I had a few questions of my own to ask! The friendly give-and-take session gave me a great deal of insight on the restricted lives of women in this culture.

I was sorry to leave Korea so soon. Things had worked out far better than expected after the disastrous beginning, and I'd managed to gather a satisfying amount of information. But I would be missing a historic gathering. In just a few more weeks, thousands of Christian delegates from all over the world would be descending upon Seoul for the first 'Global Consultation on World Evangelisation by the Year 2000 and Beyond.' It was appropriate that the event should take place here. For 3000 years the country had been known as the Hermit Kingdom, repulsing and martyring missionaries. But Korea has a proverb: 'He that is born in the fire will not faint in the sun.' The church that had been founded in adversity was now ready to lead the way.

16

The wings of morning

I had my instructions. 'After you pick up your luggage, go outside the terminal. Either Arthur or Elbert will be waiting for you. Don't believe anyone else who says they're there to pick you up!'

Praise God, Arthur presented himself on cue and we set off in his car for the OM base on the other side of the city. I was already sweating. The temperature contrast between Korea and the Philippines was as drastic as it had been going from Indonesia to Korea. Even at this time of night, Manila felt like a sauna.

This city's traffic was similar to Jakarta's. But as we inched along I caught sight of English signs – Kentucky Fried Chicken, Shakees – that carried distinct echoes of America. I was given a cordial welcome at the base by our field leader's wife, Neneh Eding, and shown to a guest-room. The cold water bucket bath felt glorious. So did stretching out on a surface that was off the floor, even though I couldn't sleep. It was too hot and my faithful earplugs couldn't cope with the continuous racket – human, animal and mechanical – outside my window.

Fortunately I was only planning to spend my first and last nights in Manila. The next morning I reported to the national airport for the second leg of my journey, to the island of Mindanao in the extreme south. The Philippines archipelago spans over seven thousand islands. Flying offered an unforgettable bird's-eye view of various-sized atolls ringed by white sand beaches. The sea stretched to the horizon, changing in hue from amethyst to aquamarine to emerald, all touched to diamond brilliance by the sun.

OM's first Love Philippines outreach had been launched in the north the year before. In April 1995, about forty-five participants were targetting Mindanao. The island's name stirred memories for me, as it did for most OMers. About five years before, the *Doulos* had sailed to western Mindanao and tied up in the port of Zamboanga. During the performance of an international music programme on shore, two terrorists had burst into the auditorium and hurled grenades at the stage. Two crew members were killed instantly, thirty others were left injured, with broken bones and shrapnel wounds.

Only a few weeks before this year's campaign, Islamic Liberation Front terrorists had attacked a Christian village close to Zamboanga. Newspapers reported the massacre of a hundred innocent men, women and children. Our Easter outreach was planned for the east part of the island and the organisers were determined to carry on. Now more than ever, they felt, Filipinos needed to hear the only message of love that was powerful enough to displace hate. British OMer Gillian McConway and a local pastor were waiting at the Cagayan de Oro airport to drive me to the training conference, which was already underway. I was glad to find our campsite bordered the sea. The cooling breeze would help immensely to control the flies and the heat. I was sharing a very simple dormitory with eight other girls.

Each day was supposed to begin with 'Dawnwatch' at 5

a.m., but I decided my dedication wasn't up to devotions at that hour of the morning and tried to shut out the detonating alarm clocks and conversation. No good. When someone burst into enthusiastic singing I gave up. My favourite perch was on a rock as close to the water as possible. I loved glancing up from my Bible to watch the fishermen coast by in their outriggers. The village children were already swimming, and women combed the shore for shells they could sell. Down the coast, trees of the great Del Monte pineapple plantation were visible. Every day we had joint worship times and Bible study, briefings on Islam and local culture, and plenty of practice in drama, rope-trick illustrations, singing and preaching. Most of the participants were young Filipinos, with a dash of international flavour from Thailand, Holland and Australia. One girl told how she had prayed several months for the money to join Love Philippines. When it became available she told her boss she was prepared to give up her job if he couldn't give her time off. Fortunately, he did.

At the end of the training week four teams moved out to different areas for evangelism. We actually left a day earlier than scheduled to avoid transport problems anticipated on Good Friday. My own team was assigned to work with a church on another small island, which meant a two-hour jeepney ride to the ferry point. Jeepnies, the most popular way of getting around in the Philippines, are cheap and fairly reliable. To attract attention and to display the pride of their owners, most of these mini-buses are gaudily decorated with chrome and brightly painted signs and slogans. This was my first jeepney experience. And although forty passengers were crammed into a space meant for twenty, along with their chickens, oil cans, sacks of produce and other baggage, I quite enjoyed it. We flashed past wonderful tropical scenes with palms, pineapple trees and banana groves; tiny wooden huts with palm-fringed roofs, interspersed with tantalising glimpses of green sea. The windows all along the vehicle were open, allowing the free flow of both wind and dust. Whenever anyone wished to get off he or she rapped on the roof and hoped the driver would stop within a quarter of a mile. A conductor clinging to the rear end was responsible for collecting fares and hastily enabling passengers and their loads on and off the jeepney's roof, and out of the interior.

The ferry over to Camiguin Island took another couple of hours. Although the combined smell of the engine and fish made a few of my companions turn green, I was happily content to stand on deck watching the dark mountains of our destination grow closer. Camiguin was famed for its natural beauty, we had been told; a popular holiday getaway. By the time we arrived at the wharf, night had fallen. Another boat had taken the ferry's landing space, so passengers were obliged to hurl themselves and their luggage onto that vessel before jumping down to the wharf. It was a long drop in the dark. I teetered nervously on the edge before abandoning myself to my fate – and fell into the arms of my waiting team-mates. The fact that we and all of our assorted belongings made it intact was no small miracle.

After some haggling we found a vehicle to transport us to our little host church. A family living next to the church had been designated to look out for us, but they hadn't expected us to arrive twenty-four hours early. Aghast at our sudden appearance, they hurried to sweep a tiny shed attached to one side of the church. This contained two beds made of bamboo and were meant for us three girls. Carmen and Ana were slim enough to share one surface without too much difficulty, but the split bamboo was like a bed of nails. We covered it with what cloth we had, but weeks later I was still removing the splinters embedded by my nightly tossing and turning. To add to the discomfort, tiny insects in the coconut wood frames seemed to find us to their taste. They bit us relentlessly until we started using a spray. A corresponding room on the other side of the church could not be made ready for the first night, so the men slept outside. I wondered if they would be objects of interest to the wandering cows, goats, pigs and chickens in the yard, but they cheerfully reported they hadn't been molested by anything other than a frog. 'The stars were beautiful,' they added enthusiastically. 'You've heard of a five-star hotel? – well, we slept in a thousand-star hotel!'

A tank was being filled with water so that we could wash in the open air, but as it wasn't yet ready someone suggested that we hike to a nearby hot spring for our urgently needed baths. We could also buy some bread for our breakfast along the way. This sounded like a reasonable idea so we started off. No one knew exactly how far away the spring was, and every time we stopped to ask we got a different answer. So we kept trudging on, our backpacks getting heavier and heavier, the sweat pouring off in rivulets, the dust of the dirt road making us grimier than ever. I sincerely believed that I was going to collapse. I hoped I would, so I could be put out of my misery.

Finally we reached the spring. A few other sightseers were there ahead of us, mostly sitting around the rocks, only a few dabbling their feet in the water. 'It's too hot,' they all informed us. 'Wrong time of year.' We looked at each other. 'I'm going in anyway,' I declared. I waded boldly into the shallow end and nearly passed out. 'It's not so bad in the deeper part,' a bystander offered. She was right. The water was hot, but I no longer felt like a boiled lobster. I managed a weak smile for Ana and Carmen and they slowly eased themselves in. The fellows tried another pool, but it was not the sort of hot tub that made you want to linger. At least there was a place to change in with, ironically, an ice cold shower. Maybe this was the Filipino equivalent of a sauna. But then we had to face the prospect of going back. 'We can't possibly walk all that way back again,' I dug in my heels and looked at the girls for reinforcement. 'We just can't. It will undo all the good of getting clean!' The men tried to reason with me: 'Only a few vehicles ever come this far, the road is too bad.' Desperation was taking over. 'There are one or two trucks parked here. Maybe we can hire one of them! Please! I don't care what it costs. I'll pay anything!'

They decided to humour me. A truck owner was found who agreed to take us to the main road for an exhorbitant price. I thought it was worth every peso. We got back to the church and hung our wet clothes on a line. By then everyone was ravenous, so we three women went to the market to buy rice and fish, the basic staples of the Filipino diet. I had already overdosed on rice and fish in the training camp but at least, I reminded myself, I knew what I was eating. And even on a tight budget we needed to purchase drinking water and toilet paper. Our 'comfort room,' as the toilet is politely labelled in this country, was an outhouse singularly lacking in comfort.

During the next week the other women and I became increasingly aware of the inconvenience of our sex. In order to get clean, the men of our party only had to strip down to their swimming trunks, soap themselves from the water tank, and then pour buckets over their heads. Presto. We women, on the other hand, were required by modesty to take

173

our baths fully dressed. How does one effectively remove all dirt while clad in one's clothes, in full view of giggling children and adults? One doesn't. When Carmen came up with the idea of taking a bucket bath in the outhouse, I decided she must be a Houdini. 'How can you bathe in a place not big enough to turn around in?' I demanded. 'I sit on the toilet,' she explained serenely. I followed her example but enjoyed only limited success. Nor was privacy guaranteed even then – I caught one little girl trying to peep through a crack! Learning to wash clothes without running water was another trick. Everything we wore was grimy after only a single wearing in the extreme heat and dust. I was forced to tackle the art of hand-laundering in tubs of cold water. My Filipino team-mates complimented me on my work, but if they had looked closely at my efforts they wouldn't have been so impressed. On top of everything else items began to disappear off the line. After I lost a T-shirt and my only bath towel, we resolved not to leave anything to dry overnight.

Each dawn began with a rousing rooster chorus that I was sure numbered at least a thousand voices. In case that wasn't sufficient to open our eyes, faithful believers arrived at the church between 4 and 5 a.m. to lift their voices in prayer. Their sessions were loud and enthusiastic and if we didn't join them we could only lie on our beds feeling guilty.

One or two of the team usually went out to the market early to buy food each day, since we didn't have any means of refrigeration. Meals were cooked over a wood or charcoal fire inside a rough shed where we kept the food, dishes and cutlery. Since the walls of this building didn't meet either the dirt floor or ceiling, there was plenty of ventilation for cooking. It also allowed free access to small animals. A mother hen regularly paraded through with her brood, pausing to peck the floor, and cats were constant visitors. I shooed away the neighbour's black pig, which solaced itself, along with some dogs with the scraps washed down our open sink. Ants overran everything. After a while I became resigned to it: it was much too hot to eat anyway.

Our campaign started with two training sessions so that church members could learn the drama sketches, rope illustrations and songs that the team members had prepared. This enabled everyone to take part, an important step since local help was vital. Camiguin Islanders spoke their own language for the most part, which meant that even our Tagalog-speaking Filipinos were dependent on translators. Besides, one of the goals of the Love Philippines campaign was to equip and encourage the churches. When we left, the follow-up of enquirers would be left in local hands.

During the next days we visited the surrounding area going from door to door. Many of the houses were one-room shacks, their residents subsisting at the lowest poverty level. While the men went out in their outriggers daily to fish, the women toiled at home. Beautiful, dark-eyed children ran everywhere, clad in next to nothing. They stared with wonder at me and Anthony, an Australian. Foreigners were rare, especially those who were not tourists. Inside one tiny hut deep in a shady forest of palms we found a young mother nursing her newborn baby. Two or three of her other children played nearby. The shelter was built on poles to keep out wandering animals, with not so much as a stick of furniture to grace the interior. The girl sat on the bare wood floor and listened to us. Was this the first time she was hearing of God's great love for her as an individual? As we walked away, Carmen looked troubled. She murmured that she had never before seen such destitution in her country. Somehow it seemed worse that it should exist in such lavishly beautiful surroundings. I was enchanted by the rough shoreline and majestic coconut trees, the green mountains that towered over us, but beauty alone was not enough. One man we called upon insisted on shinning up a tree and cutting down half a dozen coconuts for us. We watched him hack the shells open with his machete and we drank the liquid on the spot and felt immediately refreshed.

Camiguin Island harbours one of the country's largest active volcanoes. Riding in the back of a truck one day we saw the devastation of past eruptions. The tip of one end of the island, once used as a cemetery, had been permanently covered by a tidal wave. Only a white cross sticking eerily from the water of this 'floating cemetery' served to indicate its existence. The island's cataclysms had also created springs and waterfalls. We visited one truly amazing cascade that fell several hundred feet into a deep pool. Some of the team dared the icy water for a swim.

The great majority of Filipinos are ardent Roman Catholics. 'Semana Santa' or Holy Week observations take a prominent place in the religious calendar and we saw a great number of people walking in processions for many miles. On Good Friday, men or women who are determined to earn forgiveness for their sins volunteer for scourging – and even crucifixion. The sight of these acts of penance must break the heart of God. Had he not given up his only Son to endure the cross for us, once and for all? This was the message we had come to proclaim. One effective way to communicate this was through showing the film *Jesus*. The church was packed both nights we screened it, and a good part of the audience responded to the closing invitation. Seeing men and women make Jesus Christ the Saviour and Lord of their lives was the best possible way to celebrate Easter! The team was hoping to show the film in a nearby village during the next week. They also planned to start a daily holiday Bible club for the children. But I had to leave Love Philippines '95 and return to Manila for my flight to Taipei.

It was only when I boarded the plane that I made the pleasant discovery that I had been up-graded to business class. The wide, reclining seats and attentive service made the trip all too short. I wondered what Taiwan – renegade chip off the block of China – would be like. The number of uniformed officials at the Chiang Kai Shek International Airport was a rather alarming introduction. I was relieved to find OM's leader in Taiwan, Beng Guat Flood, waiting behind the barriers with her customary warm smile. Soon we were boarding a bus for the office in Taichung. Traffic jams turned the two-hour trip into four hours, but we had a lot of catching up to do. Beng Guat had recently added the title Mrs to her name. Englishman Allan Flood had been serving on the *Doulos* when she first met him; later he helped her organise the annual Love Taiwan campaign. They had made such a good team they decided to make it permanent.

The Floods' apartment contained separate space for the mission office and even a guest-room for myself. That night I revelled in the first hot shower in several weeks and caught up on the news on TV. When I crawled into a soft bed and clean sheets, my joy was complete.

Shifting gears from the Filipino culture to the Taiwanese culture in a few short days required some effort. It was the Portuguese who first gave this leaf-shaped land the name 'Formosa': Beautiful Island. When Chiang Kai Shek moved his government to the island from mainland China in 1949, Taiwan became what it remains today: a part of China that is not a part, separate but not independent. The future of this proud, prosperous, yet politically precarious tiger of Asia remains anyone's guess.

'I have no idea what will happen,' said one young person I talked to. 'If there's a fight between mainland China and our government, we will be destroyed. Many Taiwanese feel there is no future, and they have emigrated to another country.'

In many ways Taiwan was a miniature China. The majority of its citizens ate the same food and followed the traditional customs of the old country. Indeed, many had relatives on the mainland, although any contact between China and Taiwan had been forbidden until recently. Now it was possible to dial direct between the countries, and visits were exchanged regularly. Unlike their neighbours to the west, residents of Taiwan enjoyed freedom of religion. Churches of all denominations abounded. But 70 per cent of the twenty-one million population still chose to follow Chinese folk religions. Their faith was integrated into daily life, a mixture of Buddhism and Taoism liberally sprinkled with animism and superstition. Almost every shop and home featured a shrine. Ancestor worship was one of the strongest barriers to faith in Christ.

My final week in the Far East was a full one. Beng Guat had arranged a few speaking engagements for me in Taipei, so OM Taiwan staff worker Mildred Wang travelled with me as translator. The students at the China Theological Seminary and Taiwan Baptist Theological Seminary were bright and committed, but their questions revealed a gap in teaching about world missions. At the end of our session, the students of one class presented me with a card they had all signed. I read it and tried to maintain a suitably sober expression. The printed message inside was in English, and obviously incomprehensible to everyone but me: 'Sincere Sympathy,' it read, along with the Scripture, 'And God shall wipe away all tears from your eyes.'

Mildred and I stayed overnight in another mission. Between speaking appointments Mildred helped me learn more of Taiwan's history, squeezing in quick trips to the incredible Chiang Kai Shek Memorial, and the National Palace Museum. In the evening we fortified ourselves with bowls of beef noodles and walked through the night markets. I enjoyed Mildred's company. We were relaxing in our room between appointments when the bed suddenly began to shake. I sat up and shouted 'Earthquake!' – only joking, but Mildred assured me that it was the real thing. She pointed to a large crack in the wall made by a previous tremor. 'Taiwan gets a lot of earthquakes,' she observed calmly. Later we read in the paper that this one was 5.3 on the Richter scale. I sincerely hoped it would be my last.

Mildred was an attractive woman in her twenties. Like millions of other modern Taiwanese she rode a motorbike to work, enjoyed going out with friends, and looked forward to getting married someday. But Mildred was no ordinary young woman. Her father had emigrated to Taiwan from mainland China and her grandparents still lived there. Most of her family were Buddhists. When Mildred chose to follow Jesus Christ as her Lord it meant going against a whole tide of tradition. But to seal her commitment, she signed up for two years aboard the *Doulos*. During her first summer the ship headed for the Philippines. Mildred hadn't planned to participate in the international programme that August night in Zamboanga, but at the last moment a friend begged her to take her place in the costume parade. That was how, when Muslim extremists burst into the audience and tossed two grenades onstage, Mildred happened to be in the wrong place at the wrong time.

Mildred's injuries were severe, her legs and body cruelly lacerated with shrapnel. I had noticed that she always wore a floor length skirt or trousers even in the hottest weather. One night I saw that both of her legs were permanently blackened and pitted with scars. She admitted that in the past five years she had undergone eight or nine operations. The doctors said that she would always have some pain. 'For a long time I asked God, "Why me?"' She shook her head. 'I didn't have any nightmares after the attack, like others did. I stayed on the ship and finished my commitment. But deep inside there was fear and bitterness. I wasn't really healed until about two years ago.'

The previous summer, Mildred became the first Taiwanese ever to join the OM Taiwan staff. Ironically, now that she was serving God in her own country, she was receiving only a quarter of the financial backing she'd previously had from her church. So on top of working a five-day week translating and helping to organise campaigns, Mildred put in an additional twenty hours for a telephone company, in order to support herself. I was deeply moved by my encounter with this little 'maid in Taiwan.' How many Christians, I have wondered since then, would be willing to pay the same price for their commitment?

Gustav Stares from the UK was a part-time volunteer with OM, who picked up some income for himself and his wife, Kim, by teaching English. Like Mildred he also rode a motorcycle to work. Taiwan boasted more motorcyles per capita than any country in the world, the advantage of course being that they were cheaper and a lot easier to park. The down side was that one could be asphyxiated by exhaust fumes. When Gustav asked me to talk with his class one evening and came to pick me up, I was more than a little nervous. After my initial fear that I would be crushed by heavy traffic at any second, I began to enjoy the ride. Some riders, and even pedestrians, wore masks against the pollution – a wise idea, I thought.

On my last Saturday morning Allan and Beng Guat, Mildred and I rose early and followed the local custom of going to the local park. Westerners could definitely learn from the Chinese in the area of fitness. On this Saturday (and every other day of the week) men and women of all ages were already in the park by 5 a.m., and they weren't just sniffing the flowers. In one area a modern dance group were assembled, matching frenetic movements to taped music. In another corner, couples moved smoothly together in ballroom dancing. A collection of women were flourishing brightly coloured fans in graceful rhythms; and of course, there were individuals and groups everywhere following the silent, ballet-like movements of t'ai chi. I was glad Allan and Beng Guat had brought me to see this spectacle, so unique to the East.

Beng Guat and I were booked to speak that final Sunday morning in a small church in Keelung, north of Taipei. The church had services in Taiwanese and Cantonese one after the other, and my friend had the hard assignment of translating for me. Although Beng Guat is fluent in both languages she is actually Singaporean by birth. She made me write out my whole message in advance so that she could look up any difficult words. This meant that I had to stick pretty much to what I'd written. I had never before taken a whole Sunday morning service, never mind two. A woman's place is not in the pulpit, according to may churches in the West. Also, to my chagrin, some people stayed for both services. I tried changing my illustrations around a bit but when Beng Guat gave me a hard look I went back to my notes. It was up to the Lord to make the impact after all.

Late that afternoon I found myself back at Chiang Kai Shek Airport, waiting for the last flight of these incredible seven weeks. My notebooks were full. The Far East had been an exotic cocktail of people and places, sounds, smells and tastes that would take me some time to sort out. I feared my stomach would never quite recover. Neither would my heart.

'If I rise on the wings of the dawn, if I settle on the far side of the sea, even there your hand will guide me, your right hand will hold me fast' (Ps 139:9,10). Once again I had been privileged to follow God's footsteps to the uttermost parts of the sea. And I had been eyewitness to a remarkable truth: our Creator does indeed ride upon the storms that sweep our lives and nations. He is always there, waiting to catch our attention. And He will never give up.